THE SCHOOL LEADER'S
GAME PLAN

STRATEGIES FOR MAXIMIZING YOUR
CAPACITY TO TACKLE DAILY CHALLENGES

SCOTT A. LALIBERTE

Solution Tree | Press

Copyright © 2025 by Solution Tree Press

Materials appearing here are copyrighted. With one exception, all rights are reserved. Readers may reproduce only those pages marked "Reproducible." Otherwise, no part of this book may be reproduced or transmitted in any form or by any means (electronic, photocopying, recording, or otherwise) without prior written permission of the publisher. This book, in whole or in part, may not be included in a large language model, used to train AI, or uploaded into any AI system.

555 North Morton Street
Bloomington, IN 47404
800.733.6786 (toll free) / 812.336.7700
FAX: 812.336.7790

email: info@SolutionTree.com
SolutionTree.com

Visit **go.SolutionTree.com/leadership** to download the free reproducibles in this book.

Printed in the United States of America

Library of Congress Cataloging-in-Publication Data

Names: Laliberte, Scott A., author.
Title: The school leader's game plan : strategies for maximizing your
  capacity to tackle daily challenges / Scott A. Laliberte.
Description: Bloomington, IN : Solution Tree Press, 2025. | Includes
  bibliographical references and index.
Identifiers: LCCN 2024041392 (print) | LCCN 2024041393 (ebook) | ISBN
  9781962188494 (paperback) | ISBN 9781962188500 (ebook)
Subjects: LCSH: Educational leadership. | School administrators. |
  Work-life balance.
Classification: LCC LB2806 .L23 2025 (print) | LCC LB2806 (ebook) | DDC
  371.2/011--dc23/eng/20241227
LC record available at https://lccn.loc.gov/2024041392
LC ebook record available at https://lccn.loc.gov/2024041393

Solution Tree
Jeffrey C. Jones, CEO
Edmund M. Ackerman, President

Solution Tree Press
President and Publisher: Douglas M. Rife
Associate Publishers: Todd Brakke and Kendra Slayton
Editorial Director: Laurel Hecker
Art Director: Rian Anderson
Copy Chief: Jessi Finn
Senior Production Editor: Sarah Foster
Copy Editor: Jessica Starr
Proofreader: Sarah Ludwig
Text and Cover Designer: Kelsey Hoover
Acquisitions Editors: Carol Collins and Hilary Goff
Content Development Specialist: Amy Rubenstein
Associate Editors: Sarah Ludwig and Elijah Oates
Editorial Assistant: Anne Marie Watkins

This book is dedicated with love to my incredible wife Suzanne—my partner, my fellow adventurer, and my best friend. *¡La aventura espera!*

ACKNOWLEDGMENTS

No project as ambitious as a book evolves without significant influence from those surrounding the author. This is particularly true of books about leadership. We grow as leaders because of those who have led and mentored us. While the sheer number of years and the limitations of memory essentially guarantee I will omit people from this list, I would be remiss if I didn't at least attempt to acknowledge some of those leaders who have shaped my own view of leading over my years in the profession.

As such, I humbly thank the following people whose influence features prominently: Nate Greenberg, Kent Hemingway, Michael Lancor, Dr. Paul DeMinico, Sandra McGonagle, Dr. Mark Joyce, Paul MacMillan, Dr. Robert Mackin, Jean Barker, Mary Lou Cronin, and coaches William Dod, Skip Swiezynski, Phil Estes, and Bill Bowes. Many more colleagues have shaped my experiences as a leader, so please know that your omission is a matter of short space and not a lack of appreciation.

All leaders have friends with whom they can share commiserations, wild ideas, and stories, both true and embellished. Among mine, I thank Dr. Brian Blake for his support and commiseration and the perspective gained through countless deep and shallow musings shared over many years. Also, thanks to fellow recovering athlete Peter Curro for keeping me sane against all odds. Thanks to so many other friends among the school leaders across New Hampshire for helping me to keep even-keeled in the water during rough seas. We are lost without the fellowship of our work.

Thanks as well to Ellen Hume-Howard and the rest of my friends at the New Hampshire Learning Initiative, who have introduced me to a broader world. In particular, thanks to fellow Solution Tree author Jonathan Vander Els, without whom this book would not exist. His thought partnership and encouragement have been invaluable in bringing to life what was once just an interesting idea.

Naturally, I owe a great debt of gratitude to my friends from Solution Tree. I thank Douglas Rife for the opportunity to dive into this work, as well as editors Laurel Hecker and Sarah Foster for their patience and guidance with this enthusiastic but awkward new author. Thanks as well to the rest of the production team for lending your gifts to this creation.

Finally, and far from least, I thank my amazing and patient wife Suzanne for her tireless support and encouragement and my daughter Paige for so many conversations about the connections between sports and the wider world. Thanks as well for so much support to my stepdaughters Shelley, Meagan, and Jessica (with each of their significant others and little ones included in sentiment), to my father, Paul Laliberte, as well as the remaining members of the wider Laliberte family crew, and my extended Bettencourt family, among whom I am proud to call myself a new-ish member. Our individual strength is rooted in the collective support of those with whom we surround ourselves, and none are stronger than family.

I love you all, and I remain grateful for each one of you.

Solution Tree Press would like to thank the following reviewers:

Jeffrey Benson
School Consultant, Leader Coach, Author
Brookline, Massachusetts

Molly Capps
Principal
McDeeds Creek Elementary School
Southern Pines, North Carolina

Jennifer Evans
Principal of Burnham School
Cicero District 99
Cicero, Illinois

Louis Lim
Principal
Bur Oak Secondary School
Markham, Ontario, Canada

David Pillar
Assistant Director
Hoosier Hills Career Center
Bloomington, Indiana

Visit **go.SolutionTree.com/leadership** to download the free reproducibles in this book.

TABLE OF CONTENTS

Reproducibles are in italics.

ABOUT THE AUTHOR xi

INTRODUCTION. 1
    The Origins and Purpose of This Book 3
    How This Book Is Organized. 4

CHAPTER 1

Focusing on Leadership Capacity for Optimal Performance, Career Sustainability, and Wellness. . . . 7

    Looking at the State of Leadership Development 9
    Using Athletics as a Model 12
    Identifying Variables Impacting School
        Leaders' Performance. 15
    Exploring Variables That Impact
        Leadership Capacity. 19
    Questions for Reflection 22
    An Inventory of Work Challenges 24
    Identifying Your Essential Competencies 26

CHAPTER 2
Learning From Elite Athletes 29
- Exploring the Seven Traits of Athletic
  Training Programs 31
- Measuring What Matters Most 37
- Considering the Merits of a Competency-
  Based Approach 39
- Handling Public and Organizational Perception ... 44
- Questions for Reflection 46
- *Protocol for Building the Work in the Current System* ... 47

CHAPTER 3
Managing Stress Reactions 49
- Understanding Stress Reactions 51
  - Understanding Fight or Flight 53
  - Looking at Longer-Term Stressors 54
  - Examining What Makes Something Threatening ... 55
- Exploring Stress's Connection to Health and Illness ... 57
- Questions for Reflection 61
- *Understanding the Context of Your
  Stress Reactions* 63
- *A Path to Mindfulness, Authentic Reflection,
  and Self-Awareness* 68
- *Capacity Overview Graphic Organizer* 70

CHAPTER 4
Exploring Optimal Physical Preparation for Leadership 73
- Preparing for Increased Stress Response 75
- Getting Started With Exercise 77
- Choosing Healthy Foods 81
- Dealing With Sickness 84
- Spending Time Outdoors 85
- Questions for Reflection 86

Carving Out Time for Activity *88*

An Inventory of How You Are Feeling *89*

CHAPTER 5

Getting Quality Sleep and Dealing With Fatigue 91

Exploring Sleep and the Brain 94

Bringing the Brain Back to Balance Using De-Escalation 98

Dealing With Fatigue 100

Questions for Reflection 101

Sleep Hygiene Checklist *102*

CHAPTER 6

Learning About Leaders' Emotional Regulation 103

Dealing With Emotions in School 106

Staying Emotionally Healthy 109

    Self-Management and Regulation 110

    Emotional Adaptability 112

    Social Skills, Empathy, and Awareness of Others 113

    Social Needs 114

Taking Advantage of Therapeutic Support 116

Questions for Reflection 118

Using Mental Rehearsal and Simulation to Prepare for
    Escalated Emotional Response *120*

Maintaining Emotional Supports Graphic Organizer *122*

CHAPTER 7

Exploring Motivation and Volition as Vital Sources of Support 125

Realizing Your Motivation and Purpose 127

Locating Your Motivation 131

    Recovering From a Loss of Volition 133

    Adapting to Changes in Volition 134

Looking at Spirituality as an Element of Volition 135

Seeing Why Authentic Reflection Is Crucial
    to Leadership 137
  Surrounding Yourself With Your Why 139
  Questions for Reflection 141
  Uncovering Your Volition...................................... 142

CHAPTER 8

Putting It All Into Practice 145

  Using Competencies as a Practical Approach in
    a Busy Schedule 147
  Assessing Your Own Strengths and Weaknesses 150
  Using Sources of Data to Track Your Growth 153
  Finding Opportunities for Support........................... 155
  Creating Your Personal Approach to
    Meaningful Reflection................................... 157
  *Building Motivational Clarity Into Your Existing
    Evaluation Process*....................................... 159
  Building Your Practice of Authentic Reflection 161
  *A Comprehensive Planning Document for Maintaining
    Your Leadership Capacity*............................... 162

EPILOGUE..165

REFERENCES AND RESOURCES.....................167

INDEX..177

ABOUT THE AUTHOR

SCOTT A. LALIBERTE

Scott is a career educational leader, consultant, presenter, and leadership coach. He believes passionately in the impact school leaders have on both student learning and the long-term sustainability of educational systems. He has over thirty-five years of experience in schools, having spent time as a teacher, curriculum administrator, principal, and superintendent in New Hampshire. In 2022, he made a professional transition from working in schools to advancing the development of educational leaders. Scott currently works with both aspiring and practicing leaders through his consultancy, Standard Shift Consulting, LLC.

Throughout his career, Scott has demonstrated his strong belief in the impact school leadership has on student learning in different ways, ranging from his long tenure as a member of the Board of Directors at the New Hampshire School Administrators Association to his frequent professional development presentations on leader well-being and skill development. He has presented across the United States on leadership capacity and has served as a mentor to many leaders who are new to the role. Prior to writing for Solution Tree, Scott has written recreationally for many years, having published two short stories with the New Hampshire Writers' Project *Anthology of Teachers Writing*, an article for the *New Hampshire Journal of Education*, a script for a children's summer theater production of a musical, and a novel he self-published in 2006. This is his first book on the topic of school leadership.

Scott gained exposure to competitive athletics as a member of the football team at the University of New Hampshire, where he was a two-year starter on the offensive line and received all-conference honors following his senior season. He went on to share those experiences with student athletes as a football, basketball, and track coach at the high school level. He holds a strong belief in the power of cocurricular activities as a fundamental element of facilitating student growth and development.

Scott holds a bachelor of arts in English from the University of New Hampshire, a master's in education in school administration from Plymouth State University, and a certificate of advanced graduate study in educational leadership from Plymouth State University. He lives in the Lakes Region of New Hampshire with his wife Suzanne.

To learn more about Scott's work, follow @scottlalib7122 on X, scottlalib on Facebook, Scott Laliberte on LinkedIn, and scottandrew7 on Instagram.

To book Scott A. Laliberte for professional development, contact pd@SolutionTree.com.

INTRODUCTION

Do you know what it feels like to be entirely depleted? I do. My story begins in winter 2022. I was serving as superintendent in a suburban school district in southern New Hampshire while the United States was emerging from the COVID-19 pandemic. Like nearly everyone in the education profession and the world beyond, I felt empty, both in the physical and mental sense. I struggled to recenter myself with some sense of purpose and clarity, yet I found none in my daily work. I was exhausted, unhealthy, and disconnected from the sense of purpose that had driven me through thirty-two years of work in K–12 education. Something needed to change.

At fifty-five years old, I decided that dire circumstances required dire solutions, so I took an early retirement. There would be no sunbirding or full-time golf, though. I walked away from a great job in a notable career at a time when I should have had a lot more fuel left in the tank to give to my role as a systems leader. I also walked toward the next chapter in my story, whatever that would be.

I left in search of answers. What had happened to me? Yes, the pandemic was difficult for everyone, and yet many leaders have continued without the challenges I had faced. I am normally a very healthy, strong, and resilient person, yet I suddenly found myself separated from the roots of my motivation. I know I wasn't alone.

The journey that followed resulted in this book. It emerged from my attempts to understand how a healthy, capable, and motivated leader can so quickly burn out to a degree where walking away is the only apparent solution. Like most answers, this one comes with complexities and confounding variables. That said, the effort to understand my journey also made it clear that if we expect educational leaders to function at optimal levels in an environment that continues to become more complex and demanding, we must reconfigure and expand the ways in which they are prepared for their roles and how they sustain themselves within it.

School and district leaders often compartmentalize their own professional development into categories prescribed by recertification or evaluation. In their learning, they make the best of the scarce time and resources left over at the end of incredibly full days. In this book, I propose a different standard based on optimal performance and a means of working toward it even in the face of ongoing challenges. After all, most educational leaders seek a path toward consistent and sustainable work at the upper limits of our personal abilities. Leaders want to be as effective as they can be each day. In this book, I propose that this is only possible if you, as a leader, take active steps to positively impact your physical health, cognitive functioning, and emotional well-being, and ensure that you have a clear sense of what motivates you. Therefore, you must structure the means of sustaining yourself—not out of a well-intended commitment to a wider sense of wellness but because optimal functioning is at the root of performing leadership responsibilities.

This book investigates the variables that support reaching optimal performance levels. It looks at what educational leaders can do differently in professional development to minimize or counteract these factors. This book explores what's possible when structuring a leadership development program around optimizing performance instead of only focusing on pockets of content knowledge. It is intended for a full range of experience levels of educational leaders—from those educators entering into the leadership profession to those already well down the path.

Let's begin by looking at an area that is highly developed and familiar to many educational leaders—competitive athletics—where training programs are highly specialized and personalized, encompassing any pertinent variable that can impact an athlete's ability to perform at optimal levels. There is much to learn from those techniques used by athletes both before and during competition. The book explores seven core traits shared by competitive athletes' training programs and then applies them to the world of school and systems leadership. These traits are not exhaustive but instead form a link to the work of educational leaders. The following are seven traits of athletic training programs that can be applied to leadership development.

1. Managing physiological stress reactions
2. Addressing physical, mental, emotional, and motivational variables that impact performance levels

of one's breathing and levels of arousal allow for greater muscular pliability and decreased injury. Although many of these concepts were novel at that time, they have become the norm in contemporary training programs for elite athletes (Martin, 2023; Velocity Sports Performance, 2021).

I fully embraced these concepts as a college athlete and managed to experience levels of relative success above my natural athletic ability. Over time, I found similar performance parallels in my career as an educational leader.

Connecting leadership to athletics is nothing new. Any reader with experience in both worlds has no doubt made that mental leap at one time or another. That said, this book aspires to push that connection further into a foundational application of effective training practices.

This book is not a comprehensive how-to manual, nor is it intended to be a completely new model of professional development for leaders. Instead, it offers a framework for an expanded definition of what it takes for leaders to perform at the outer limits of their individual potential. The intent is for readers to come away with a starting point and personalized direction on how they can best build their leadership capacity. Leaders will implement daily practices and active steps to improve their physical well-being, cognitive functioning, emotional balance, and motivational clarity in ways that are connected to their larger leadership development efforts.

It is the beginning of a new and better path for leaders who are seeking to continuously grow despite the considerable challenges that face them. Leaders may not be able to change the stressful nature of their work, but they can better prepare themselves to thrive within it.

How This Book Is Organized

This book is constructed in a progression that begins with a broader examination of current leadership development efforts and continues into a look at the broader elements available to school leaders for developing their capacity to function within their work's challenges. With the component parts identified, the book progresses into more specific, implementable strategies for applying athletic training traits to the growth and sustenance of school leaders over time. Each chapter concludes with reproducible tools that allow leaders to develop personalized approaches to their own efforts to maintain capacity.

3. Exploring training that is specialized to sport and personalized to athlete
4. Managing physical, cognitive, and emotional energy
5. Using simulation and mental rehearsal
6. Maintaining motivational clarity, which is a clear connection between what you are doing and why you are doing it
7. Using dynamic game planning by planning, planning to adapt, and adapting

This book explores what it takes for leaders to function at optimal levels by examining the impact of stress on our bodies and minds and considering variables affecting performance, including physical health, cognitive functioning, and emotional regulation. Since making this work less stressful is simply not realistic, efforts at professional growth and optimal performance need to focus on better preparing leaders to endure the stress. Just as elite athletes train for competition, leaders can train for their work as well. The outcome is a broader, competency-based approach to leadership development that encompasses pertinent factors that affect leaders performing at the outer limits of their potential.

The Origins and Purpose of This Book

In the late 1980s, as a member of the University of New Hampshire football team, I had the good fortune to participate in a pilot program for what was then termed a *mental conditioning program*. This program challenged participants to expand their working knowledge of training principles beyond conventional topics. At that time, I had no idea what such a program might entail, yet that experience shaped much of my thinking as a student athlete and as a leader of school systems.

The principle was elegant in its simplicity. For an athlete to perform at the outer limits of their ability, they should include elements of training and preparation that reach all possible variables associated with their performance. It isn't enough to focus solely on physical strength or tactical knowledge. Most athletes are aware that performance is affected by their mental approach, the ways they encounter the stress of competition, and their core physiological health habits, such as sleep and recovery. Therefore, a successful approach to training for competition should address each of these concepts and more. For example, the program asserted that positive visualization and mental rehearsal lead to replicable success. And the modulation

Chapter 1 looks at the current state of leadership preparation and at the potential that can be found in a broader definition of leadership capacity as opposed to discrete skills and abilities. This book considers the full range of conditions that impact leaders' performance each day—from those traditionally accounted to those that may escape notice. Mental and physical fatigue, emotional challenges, cognitive overload, and motivational disillusionment all impact how leaders work in a given moment, yet are often overlooked in relation to professional growth and job performance.

Chapter 2 looks at the world of competitive athletics and the ways in which the previously mentioned seven common traits of training and preparing for competition might apply to your work as leaders. Here you'll explore specific circumstances for each trait as it applies to each chapter.

Chapter 3 examines the stress response and the ways it impacts leaders, both positively and negatively. The sympathetic nervous system presents common reactions to stress—and yet the perception of stress varies widely. This variance is why each leader needs the freedom to facilitate their own development in a manner that best suits them.

Chapter 4 observes how school leaders might best prepare themselves for the physical demands of their stressful work. In considering the effect of frequent or prolonged activation of the stress response, elements such as cardiovascular health, the positive impact of exercise, and the value of an individualized approach to diet are all considered part of the process for developing a substantive approach to capacity building.

Chapter 5 discusses information regarding cognitive functioning. In specific, this chapter looks at the importance of quality sleep and an intentional de-escalation of the stress response. Both become integral elements of a leader's ability to think clearly, apply sound judgment to complex situations, and balance the many divergent cognitive demands that make up their day-to-day work.

Chapter 6 delves into the emotional demands of leading schools and the challenges that are specific to the various roles. It examines the foundations of emotional well-being, as well as strategies for approaching some of the typical yet complicated emotional elements of life through the unique lens of a school leader. Often times leaders provide significant emotional support to those within their schools, yet they neglect their own care in life's challenging moments.

Chapter 7 examines the most important element of performance, which is motivation. The chapter investigates the roots of our own volition—the basis on which leaders make decisions in the day to day, as it applies to their overall sense of purpose.

Like competitive athletes, these ideals push leaders through difficult times and keep them working at the outer limits of their abilities.

Chapter 8 helps each reader construct a realistic, personalized plan to maintain their leadership capacity within the circumstances in which they lead.

At the conclusion of chapters 1–7, you will find Questions for Reflection sections that will allow you to personalize the concepts covered in each chapter. The value of authentic reflection and the personalization of your professional learning are both emphasized throughout the book, and these questions will set you on a path toward both outcomes. Regardless of your current professional learning model, stage of life or career, or experience leading school buildings or educational systems, I invite you to explore your own path to optimal performance and capacity. In addition, reproducibles provide various activities to help you develop your leadership capacity.

My modest wish for every reader is that you come away with a different perspective on what it takes to sustain yourself and grow as a leader. Don't discard those variables that connect directly to your capacity to lead, thinking of them as some form of luxury or void in your schedule. Give yourself the license to think deeply, reflect authentically, and advance aggressively those components that most directly impact the development of your own personal leadership capacity. Those elements compose the road by which you will continue to grow, thrive, and work at the outer limits of your potential, despite the considerable challenges leaders face.

CHAPTER 1

FOCUSING ON LEADERSHIP CAPACITY

FOR OPTIMAL PERFORMANCE, CAREER SUSTAINABILITY, AND WELLNESS

Using Athletics as a Model

Like all cocurricular programs, athletic programs are included in school offerings as an important part of student learning. Among many other attributes, these programs offer students an opportunity to learn the value of collaboration, commitment, and work ethic; strategies for performing under pressure; and a sense of self within the constructs of a larger team. As such, athletics assumes a pivotal role in the larger atmosphere of learning in formalized schooling. Therefore, it is little wonder that leaders turn to some of the best ideas associated with athlete development to discover new and more substantive approaches to preparing and sustaining school leaders.

Many school leaders find common roots in their own participation in athletic programs, whether as competitors, coaches, or both. They cite those experiences as formative to their identities as leaders and to the principles that guide their thinking in their chosen roles. While this certainly does not suggest that all school leaders need be former athletes or even interested in athletics, this book is committed to coalescing the common experiences of those leaders into a substantive approach for developing and sustaining the capacity required to work at optimal levels.

The work of school leaders is too important and too demanding to leave any valuable resource unexamined.

Where leadership preparation typically follows an academic model punctuated by content area standards, little attention is paid to the broader development of individual leader's performance capacity. What would a leadership development model look like if it focused on sustained performance at optimal levels? I think such a model would land closer to the development of elite competitive athletes.

Unfortunately for leaders, exhaustion, burnout, and frustration have become normalized. According to a 2023 article in Forbes, "Nearly half (46%) of district superintendents planned to leave within two or three years" (Perna, 2023). In this article, the author continues on, in a conversation with Learning A–Z President Lisa O'Masta, to identify administrators working "long hours with immense workloads," as well as "politicization of the classroom, intensified scrutiny, and increased engagement from the community" as the sources of this trend (Perna, 2023). In the face of these challenges, the weight of expanded responsibility and the resulting conflicts that are becoming inherent in leading schools continue to increase. There is little hope of that trend reversing in the foreseeable future.

These expanded responsibilities and deepening challenges make perfect sense relative to the fundamental purpose of school systems. Schools exist primarily to prepare young people for the demands of citizenship in a larger world; that world is becoming more complex by the day, and leaders can only expect the work to evolve as well. Demands for deeper application of knowledge, the ability to evaluate the credibility of information, and a dynamic approach to learning and implementing new knowledge are just a few of the challenges that confront school leaders each day as they design learning experiences that prepare students for the world that awaits them. The work isn't getting any easier; therefore, it becomes even more important to reexamine the ways leaders prepare themselves to carry it out.

This chapter examines potential changes that come from a different perspective on leading and the importance of a more personalized approach to both the entry into leadership and the ongoing development of practicing leaders. First, the chapter establishes the current state of leadership development in schools. Then, it discusses the case for moving from leadership development to focusing on building leadership capacity to improve performance. Next, it identifies variables that impact school leaders' performances. Finally, it explores variables that affect leadership capacity.

Looking at the State of Leadership Development

School leadership demands energy, and the process of sustaining energy comes from the system of support that surrounds you. So, where do these systems of support come from? A study conducted by the RAND Corporation confirms that while support is available to leaders, it is widely inconsistent and varied by district (Johnston, Kaufman, & Thompson, 2016). Although districts do recognize the importance of leadership development, it remains incumbent on individual leaders to seek support and learning opportunities where they need them.

As for the more formalized systems of professional learning and support, these remain much the same since the 1970s. For the most part, traditional methods of leadership preparation are rooted in three fundamental areas.

1. **An academic model that is present in higher education:** This model is bracketed by academic disciplines and specialties that define content and quantify progression through earned credits.

2. **Professional standards, established through leadership organizations, that are intended to create a clear and uniform structure for the practice of leadership:** These standards bring with them consistent expectations in practice and a clear picture of the sheer breadth of expectations for leaders. Many articulate levels of performance but stop short of facilitating implementation (National Policy Board for Educational Administration, 2015).

3. **Internal or systems-specific means of orientation and succession that exist within the processes and traditions of local organizations, school districts, or professional associations:** For example, school systems are developed largely on the expectations of the communities they serve. In kind, community expectations extend to those charged with leading those systems.

These roads to leadership were established over time and formalized through interaction with one another and with a need for new talent to enter the profession (figure 1.1). These are the typical ways you become a leader in the world of education. All are well intended and serve important purposes in leadership preparation. At the point of implementation, these expectations are built around a variety of learning experiences and means of assessing leaders.

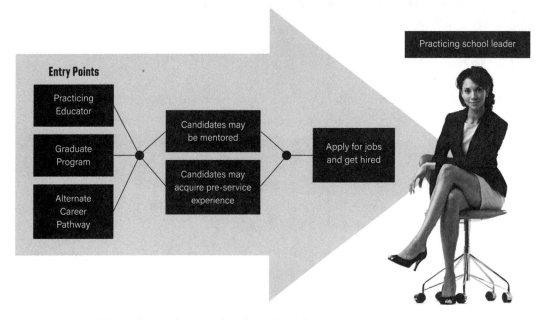

FIGURE 1.1: The paths to school leadership.

The programs shown in figure 1.1 support consistent acquisition of content knowledge, a formalized system of entry into leadership, and a systemic approach to mentorship. So, what is missing?

A few key components are not emphasized in most conventional professional learning programs for either aspiring or practicing leaders. The following elements form a barrier to entrance into the profession and a potential early exit for those already doing the work.

- **Lack of personalization:** Only marginal consideration is given to the full range of variables affecting leaders' performance within the role, and little consideration is given to leaders' current levels of aptitude and experience in facilitating their development.

- **Increasing and broadening demands:** Time and energy are focused on a wide array of content-specific knowledge and skills with little allowance for areas where the leader has already demonstrated competency. This is particularly true in K–12 school systems, where leaders function in environments that are becoming more complex, are facing greater and more diverse challenges, and are assuming a broader scope of responsibilities within the larger society.

- **Need for authentic assessment of performance, progress, and learning:** Professional assessment is often pro forma and lacks direct connection to the next steps in a leader's development. Carefully structured and specific metrics can produce assessment data that are both personalized and actionable.

- **Need for remediation and support:** Interventions for struggling leaders are typically administered in a reactive fashion, if at all. That said, failure is a part of the learning process and creates an opportunity for growth if it occurs in a reflective and restorative environment.

- **Fractured focus:** Many leadership development programs exist for specific phases of a leader's career—that is, induction or career exploration, graduate study, or career advancement—instead of in a more comprehensive system of ongoing learning that spans the entirety of a leader's career. The development of leadership skills occurs continuously and cumulatively over the course of a career or even a lifetime. Most leadership development programs support specific episodes of that timeline, not the entire arc of a leader's tenure.

National standards and academic programs form the backbone of many models of leadership development. These models have served the profession well for many years and are responsible for the high level of leadership that has become a hallmark of K–12 education. That said, as leadership challenges continue to become more comprehensive, complex, and demanding on those who choose to lead, the development methods for leaders must adapt to support their success in this environment. This observation is becoming increasingly common in school leadership literature. For example, "Leadership that is increasingly embedded within the organizational fabric, to effectively thrive in change, must be adept at building organizational capacity through continuous learning and innovation" (Winton, Palmer, & Hughes, 2018, p. 162). In many cases, more intricate elements of professional growth are left to the individual leader, even when successful growth in these areas is dependent on external support or resources.

The answers won't be found in the minutia of specific expectations, knowledge, or experiences. To see it, you must step backward to assess the broader landscape of those many wide-ranging variables that affect your work.

Using Athletics as a Model

What if a leadership development program was based on the notion of preparing for and sustaining leaders' levels of performance at the outer limits of their potential instead of fitting the work into the neat categories of existing programs built on academic disciplines? What if this program looked at the broader challenges of leading schools and built an approach around them that fortified the limitations of human performance? What could such a program look like?

First, the program would be personalized. It would begin with a thoughtful assessment of each individual leader's present condition and match methods that support them in their work. Second, it would be ongoing. As days and years passed, this program would evolve with the person engaged in it. Yes, there would be signposts, but the larger road would guide them from their entrance into leadership until their exit from it. It would recognize and build on their existing competencies in a manner measured by learning instead of time. Finally, the program would be comprehensive. It would be based on all variables that impact the performance of the leader in their role. It would be based on preparing the leader for the wide-ranging challenges that compose their days.

Were you to create such a program, it would require that you surrender some of the conventional notions of leadership preparation in its contemporary sense. A focus on capacity requires more than a graduate program or a mentorship, although they could be elements of a broader picture. However, they would become discrete elements rather than outcomes in and of themselves.

In forming a context for such a program, look at other similar areas of performance development. For example, what if there are already programs in other areas that take a more comprehensive approach to the development of performance capabilities at the outer limits of one's abilities? You need only look at the world of athletic competition.

Athletic competition has bred a deep commitment to the process of finding the outer limits of performance. There are many significant comparisons to the work of school leaders, many of which you'll explore throughout this book to gain insights into how best to develop a sustainable approach to leadership development.

Just as both performance levels and standards evolve in sports, so do expectations of leaders. As leadership has become more demanding since 2020, the methods used to prepare and support leaders need to reflect those new conditions. The following are some parallels between training for competitive sports and preparing for leadership roles.

- **Programs are differentiated to match required outcomes:** These differentiations are based on the sport, event, or position so the preparation matches the variables.
    - For example, within track and field, the athletes' training programs are different for those participating in throwing events than for sprinters or jumpers. Athletes optimize physical elements that will advance their performance.
- **Personalization and specialization based on existing skill sets determine the most appropriate role (sport and competitor):** Sports require specific skill sets and aptitudes common both to the demands of the game and to positions or roles within it. Those skill sets provide a framework for participants that guides their preparation, training, and participation in that sport. Personalized preparation becomes key to advancing within a sport.
    - For example, height, speed, lateral quickness, hand-eye coordination, and arm strength determine the most appropriate positions in the field for baseball or softball players. Once placed in the most appropriate positions, training programs provide specialized enhancement of their given skill sets.
- **There is a broad range of focus areas for training activities (not limited by convention):** Athletes use a wide range of actions that simulate a physiological element of their sport. The focus is on the development of variables impacting performance, even if that action would not be expected as part of a training program.
    - For example, the concept of cross-training has become commonplace in training plans. In some cases, this involves using other sports to train for a specific skill, such as basketball players playing tennis or racquetball to improve lateral quickness. In other cases, athletes use unique but intentional movements, such as flipping a large

tractor tire end over end to increase leg and core strength and explosiveness.

- **Expectations seldom decrease:** Where the demands of optimal performance generally increase as time passes, training aims to facilitate work at the outer limits of an athlete's abilities. Increases in performance result in increases in expectation.
  - For example, in 1925, the world record for running a marathon hovered near two hours and thirty minutes, where today's record is at the two-hour mark and elite runners regularly complete the race in two hours and fifteen minutes (Calvert, 2024). The distance has remained the same at 26.2 miles, but performance has increased dramatically.

In athletics, as in leadership, the goal is always to optimize performance within your given role. Like athletes, you seek to work at the outer limits of your capacity. How good can you be within you role? You might not be able to change the mountain, but you can be better prepared to climb it.

The single element that separates the training programs of elite athletes from those found either in history or in mediocrity is the willingness to examine all possible variables impacting their performance (J. Dana, personal communication, July 17, 2023). The goal or desired outcome in sports is relatively clear: to win. Therefore, find the outer limits of your abilities and live there. That said, achieving peak levels of performance on a consistent basis comes down to identifying all the factors that can improve performance. Sometimes, these variables are predictable and conventional, and other times they are well beyond convention. For example, the speed at which a person runs relies on the conditioning of their fast-twitch muscle fiber, muscular development in the legs and abdomen, running form, mental perseverance, and even footwear or surface. To find the outer limits of their abilities, an athlete must be willing to be creative and analytical in looking for the optimal combination of all variables. They can't change the demands of their sport or other competitors' performance levels, but they can focus on their own preparation.

Elite athletes learn early to broaden their view of physical, mental, emotional, and motivational variables that contribute to their abilities. They collect pertinent data that give them information regarding high-leverage techniques that will move the needle in these areas. They customize their preparation and training, even if that includes nontraditional approaches. Each step, no matter how minor, represents an increase in their performance level. By taking this wider view of variables impacting their performance, they identify training regimens that focus their time and resources on areas of greatest impact. The result is a detail-oriented and personalized training experience that focuses on the development of high-leverage skills. Through this approach, athletes develop specific skills and aptitudes that sustain them through the demands of competition at the highest levels. School leaders can do this too.

The following example from the world of competitive sports shows why it is beneficial to focus on performance variables:

> There has been a dramatic change in the way competitive athletes train and prepare over the past thirty to forty years. Where once the approach was to simulate competition as closely as possible and to break down performance into component parts, now there is a broader focus on overall variables impacting performance. For example, the transition in college and professional football has become evident in the change from simulating live contact game conditions in practice to the use of fitness monitors, heart rate, GPS trackers monitoring performance standards, and so on to track levels of exertion while limiting contact during practices. Full contact and simulated game conditions during practice are one way to prepare, but it brings with it the same risks of injury and long-term energy depletion that comes with live competition. Instead of simulating live game conditions, coaches now focus on physical preparation, endurance, strength, and speed, while minimizing the risk of injury during practice. This allows athletes to maintain health and strength over a prolonged season while focusing on performance variables such as technique and strategy. (J. Dana, personal communication, July 17, 2023)

Identifying Variables Impacting School Leaders' Performance

To see the full range of variables within a leader's performance, begin by broadening the scope to include factors that impact how you think, feel, and operate within school leader roles. All elements of a person's well-being can impact how they function within a leadership role. If you focus just on the job-specific skills and abilities expected of a leader, you miss a significant number of those variables. Instead, you can address a wider range of intra- and interpersonal variables that affect how you work. For the purposes of this examination, this comprehensive functioning is referred to as *leadership capacity* to distinguish it from the more traditional term of *leadership abilities* encompassed by traditional academic and standards-based definitions of leadership skills. While the term *leadership capacity* has been used in a wide range of ways, in this context it refers to the broader range of factors impacting leadership performance.

Leadership capacity includes such variables as physical health and well-being, cognitive clarity, and emotional regulation. These elements of your personal makeup clearly impact performance within the context of your professional role. You aren't at your best if you are physically ill or emotionally preoccupied to a degree that prohibits appropriate reactions within your job responsibilities. That said, these elements are rarely, if ever, discussed within the scope of traditional leadership development programs. They are acknowledged anecdotally and often informally when leaders are off in one of these areas. People are sometimes sympathetic, though rarely is there any sort of substantive address.

This is not to say that the education profession has completely neglected the wellness of school leaders. There have been many well-intended initiatives aimed at maintaining health. Whether through health insurance incentives or employee-wellness initiatives, school leaders are presented with opportunities to emphasize healthy living. Complications arise in how priorities are set. School leaders generally consider others before themselves because they have work to do, responsibilities to uphold, and a full calendar to keep. The first task to fall off your to-do list is your own health and wellness. After all, you can't possibly take time out of your day to exercise when you already have a fourteen-hour day.

So, the real limitations come from the way you frame those variables. School leaders see these capacity-preserving activities as being superfluous and expendable. How might that be different if, instead of framing your physical, cognitive, and emotional functioning as add-on elements to your day, you considered them as what they are—central to your ability to perform your responsibilities at the outer limits of your capacity?

In the chapters that follow, you will be invited to consider your physical, cognitive, and emotional well-being as integral to your ability to work at the outer limits of your potential as a school leader rather than as an optional element of your schedule. It is a subtle shift in thinking, but it could improve your work in the day to day and your longevity as a leader in schools.

What does strength look like for school leaders? While it is important to demonstrate behavior that contributes positively to the tone of a situation, that doesn't necessarily justify a long-term adherence to a romanticized notion of strength or bravery. The same can be said of the sense of selflessness that calls you to leadership positions.

As stated previously, as a school leader, you likely think of your own well-being long after the well-being of those you are responsible for. However, you are also a role model for health and well-being.

Therefore, the mindsets you adopt also impact both your behaviors and the examples you set for others. Leaders are role models with the best intentions, yet there are mindsets that you embody on a regular basis that work in contrary to the kind of self-care that is central to performing at optimal levels. In the fast-paced work of running a school or district, leaders often adopt and endorse mindsets that appear practical and noble. However, beneath each of them dwells a variable that works against the leader's intent to work at their best. Here are a few of the more common thought patterns that can negatively impact a leader's long-term capacity to lead at the outer limits of their abilities.

1. **Push through the challenges:** Yes, strength and resilience are positive expectations of an effective leader, but there are limits. It is possible to push through moments or situations while later reflecting on how that resilience emerges as a pattern. Resilience is admirable, but without ongoing and authentic reflection, it can become a detrimental pattern of unaddressed issues and repressed conflict.

2. **Internal variables such as physical health and cognitive functioning are extraneous:** School leaders often neglect their own well-being in deference to a full schedule. Think of any time you might have said or heard another leader say, "I don't have time to exercise or eat a healthy meal." This is not a sustainable mindset. Prioritizing health can save you time in the long run, principally in the form of more efficient performance.

3. **Suffering and sacrifice are necessary parts of leadership:** Suffering establishes a priority for resilience; negative outcomes are expected to be mandatory, thus outside of your control. Many leaders assume their roles expecting to make sacrifices. They see the difficulties in the work of those who came before them, and they are prepared to replicate the experience with that as a backdrop. Leadership often brings with it considerable priorities and obstacles, but leaders are in control of how they prepare for these challenges and how they experience them. Maintaining the ability to exert control over these challenges will create long-term sustainability in the leadership role, which is also a sign of a competent leader. Given that, leaders can then either mitigate

or prepare themselves for challenges rather than simply accepting them and their impact on long-term health and performance.

4. **Basic physical health and fitness are luxuries and signs of lesser commitment:** This mindset is more a product of public perception than it is of an actual ethic. There are negative voices in your communities that may criticize you for taking time out of your schedule to practice a healthy lifestyle or self-care. However, a leader taking time to exercise or to practice some other form of health maintenance is not a sign of ample free time or a lack of commitment to the work. It shows a deeper understanding of the concept of capacity and the way it impacts effectiveness.

5. **Emotional challenges, particularly outside of work, are to be stifled or hidden:** While there are higher expectations of leaders relative to emotional regulation, there is also a higher demand placed on school leaders when it comes to maintaining a healthy balance in life outside of work. Many leaders work to maintain a separation between the stressors of their jobs and those of their families, though that can often be difficult when those stressors accumulate. Part of maintaining a positive and productive workplace is acknowledging and accommodating those elements of their personal lives that impact their work. While it is possible to do so and maintain a healthy separation between home and work, it is also a means of recognizing and addressing events that may be disruptive.

Self-awareness is an important element for functioning at the outer limits of your ability. By recognizing the impact that mindsets—such as the ones discussed here—have on the capacity to function within professional responsibilities, leaders create opportunities to address challenges in a proactive manner and provide their staff with an example of prioritizing optimal functioning. Rather than accepting the long-term wear of the work as a by-product of the role, leaders include life elements that will help them endure it.

The reproducible, "An Inventory of Work Challenges" (page 24), invites readers to help contextualize this broader concept by rating the overall impact of different symptoms or factors that could impact their capacity. The objective is to increase awareness of the different ways these conditions impact work performance.

Exploring Variables That Impact Leadership Capacity

With the concept of capacity being central to your ability to perform at optimal levels as a leader, begin by establishing a framework to view the different components of performance in a clear and practical way. Start by examining the concept of capacity through the following lenses.

1. **Physical well-being:** Your ability to work at the outer limits of your potential often relies on your state of physical health (including fundamental bodily functions and habits to remain healthy). While not all elements of health are within your control, you can focus your attention on elements that are.

2. **Cognitive functioning and mental clarity:** Effective leadership of any kind relies on the leader being able to think clearly, analytically, and reflectively, even under stressful situations. The ability to maintain composure and to apply problem-solving strategies relies on a working awareness of how the brain responds to different conditions. Not only does this include knowledge of the circumstances in which you work, but also of how you personally respond to different conditions (for example, knowing if your attention span is short when you are hungry). By identifying variables where you have control, you can deploy strategies that optimize cognitive functioning even when times get tough.

3. **Emotional balance and health:** The responsibilities of leadership demand a higher degree of emotional regulation. As a leader, you are responsible for the emotional tone of situations within your organization. Often, this means that you must restrain your initial (or even authentic) emotional reaction to a situation. You must regulate your reactions to the expected scope of your responsibilities given the needs of those you lead and maintain a productive environment in your organization. In addition, you bring the regular demands of life beyond your leadership responsibilities, making it difficult to balance your broader scope of emotional well-being in your life outside of work. While these requirements are a part of your work, they also take a toll on your emotional well-being over the long term. Planning for

appropriate emotional support and healthy outlets are both important to maintaining your capacity.

4. **Motivational clarity:** School leaders have each been called to leadership roles based on some source of motivation that stems from their experiences or values. As you move through the daily challenges of your leadership roles, it is easy to become disconnected from this source of motivation. You can become pragmatic in the fullness of your days. However, there is a tremendous value in remaining connected in an intentional way to what drives you, which demands self-discipline and a commitment to authentic reflection (in whatever form that takes for you). A working awareness of your volition can help sustain you in the face of challenges that are a part of leadership.

5. **Position-specific skills and attributes:** None of these prior areas are intended to minimize the value of conventional content knowledge that is part of leadership preparation or ongoing training. Of course, leaders must know and be able to do certain tasks within the scope of their work. Much of these materials are spelled out in detail in existing leadership standards, curricula for educational programs, and district-specific expectations. These materials continue to form the backbone of what leaders do on a day-to-day basis and will form a key element of your treatment of leadership capacity.

Figure 1.2 outlines what a capacity-based leadership development model might look like if it were developed with a competency-based mindset. In the figure, the four elements identified earlier are included as *internal competencies*, which are ideas that are not commonly part of many leadership development efforts. Including them in such a model gives them weight that substantiates a commitment of time and resources to leader development. Conventional topics for leadership development are included as *external competencies* that are still of great value. This approach allows for a broader range of variables as previously outlined but maintains the ability for participants to focus on higher-leverage skills. It integrates smoothly with almost any professional learning model.

This model builds off the existing components of professional development, located in the two external competencies areas, yet adds elements that address the internal competencies that go largely unaddressed in conventional programs. As you will see as the book unfolds, this is only possible when accommodation is made in time and resources allow for additional variables to be addressed. Leaders can't simply do

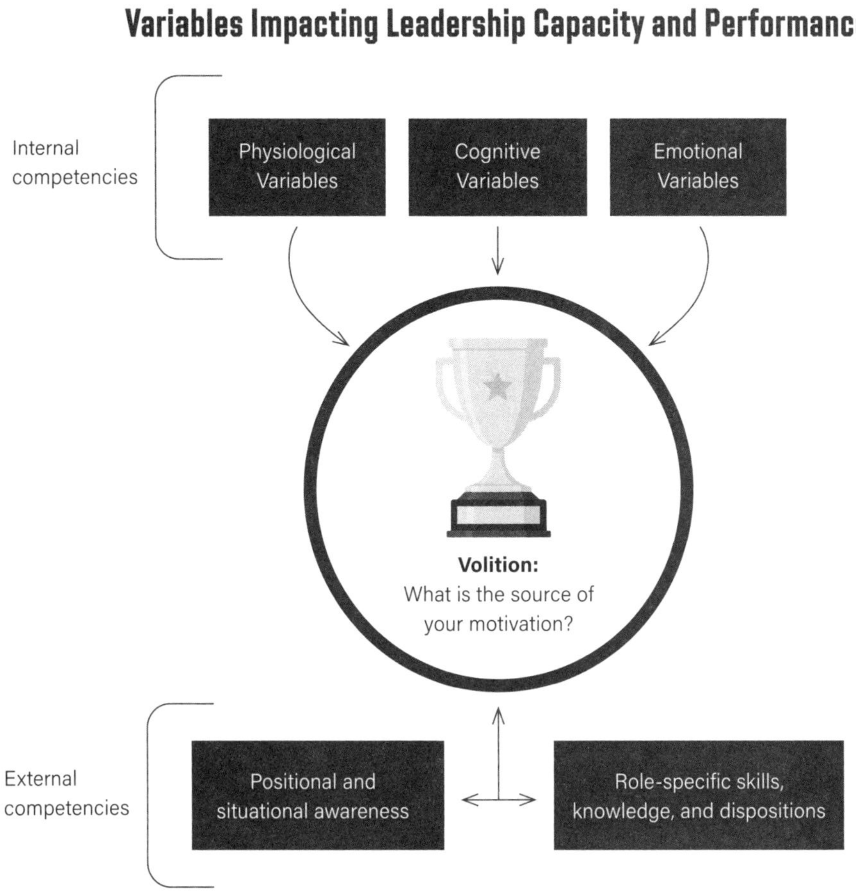

Variables Impacting Leadership Capacity and Performance

Internal competencies:
- Physiological Variables
- Cognitive Variables
- Emotional Variables

Volition: What is the source of your motivation?

External competencies:
- Positional and situational awareness
- Role-specific skills, knowledge, and dispositions

FIGURE 1.2: Competency-based leadership development.

more with the same amount of time and resources. Addressing internal competencies allows for expanded capacity and, with it, the ability to gain greater progress in current external competencies. No less significant, the intentional address of volition as the connection between all competencies gives us a clear focus on the variables that impact such issues as burnout and disillusionment, which commonly impact leaders' effectiveness.

With this structure in mind, consider the practical matters associated with implementation. Obviously, such a broad approach to leadership development would be overwhelming to practitioners with already jam-packed schedules. Instead of approaching these areas as a checklist that must be completed in full, they can form a scaffold for reflection. Many districts use goal-setting and evaluation forms that are indexed to performance expectations specific to their district. Each school district also typically establishes their own standards for leadership development with original internal expectations and others referencing a preexisting model. Rather than having leaders complete every element of these forms, supervisors could facilitate a review of these performance expectations.

By helping leaders examine those factors impacting their performance, they could come away with areas of focus that bring the greatest potential impact to their work. You aren't meant to complete all these things each year. You are meant to use them to discover what you need most in finding the outer limits of your abilities. In this interest, the concept lends itself naturally to a competency-based approach. You focus your attention on what you are ready to learn next or on what skills you need to add to your practice to maintain optimal performance levels. For example, if a leader excels at operational functions but struggles in the process of evaluating professional staff, their time and attention are dedicated to developing the weakness. The leader reflects on the full range of elements and then builds the next steps in their development around areas of greatest need or potential impact. They are then assessed by what they demonstrate within the context of their work. This concept forms a foundational element of what you will develop with this book and the strategies you will use to sustain that work.

The goal of this broader address of leadership is to consider a full range of variables that impact performance. This thought process is clearly unconventional in concept and is challenging to implement in educational leaders' daily lives. That said, the time has come for bolder steps in developing new leaders and sustaining those already in practice. If you are to achieve different results, you must begin by thinking differently.

The reproducible, "Identifying Your Essential Competencies" (page 26), provides you with an opportunity to focus on areas of greatest need and opportunity relative to your current leadership capacity.

Questions for Reflection

Use the following questions to help you reflect on what you have read in this chapter.

1. What are the greatest limitations that you recognize in your own leadership capacity? What gets in the way of you performing at your highest level?

2. Have you had any athletic experiences that shape your practice as a school leader? If so, how might those experiences be enhanced or expanded?

3. What professional learning resources or experiences are currently missing from your efforts to develop and grow as a leader?

4. What mindsets or beliefs do you recognize in yourself that could serve both as advantages and disadvantages?

5. Does your current system for monitoring professional development or recertification allow for any flexibility or personalization? If so, do you make use of it? If not, what other learning programs might allow for more personalized learning?

An Inventory of Work Challenges

This activity includes an overview of the different challenges encountered in your professional life with the intent of establishing potential areas of focus for planning. The following chart presents you with a list of some of the greatest challenges that leaders face today. Use this tool to rate the impact that each challenge has on your daily work, from 0 to 4. Use the results to prioritize the different elements of your planning in subsequent activities.

While this exercise is intended to help you determine priorities for maintaining your overall leadership capacity, it is by no means exhaustive or diagnostic. In reviewing your answers, see if you can determine a pattern that indicates whether your most significant challenges are physical, cognitive, emotional, or motivational in nature. Use this analysis to guide you in prioritizing subsequent work.

Impact	0 No Impact	1 Minimal	2 Periodic	3 Frequent	4 Constant
Physical illnesses not resulting in time out of work					
Physical illnesses resulting in lost work time					
Chronic or frequently recurring fatigue					
Chronic pain or ongoing health conditions					
Digestive distress or stomach issues					
Sleep disruption resulting in fatigue or distractedness					
Difficulty maintaining attention to tasks					
Irritability or short temper					
Difficulty maintaining a healthy body composition					
Diminished physical strength or endurance					
Cognitive fogginess or difficulty with focus					

page 1 of 2

The School Leader's Game Plan © 2025 Solution Tree Press • SolutionTree.com
Visit **go.SolutionTree.com/leadership** to download this free reproducible.

Feelings of loneliness or disconnectedness					
Use of chemical substances to manage well-being					
Frustration with current role or job responsibilities					
Feeling a lack of purpose or fulfillment in work					
Overall disconnectedness or dissatisfaction with work role					
Other challenges not mentioned here					

Using the information you gleaned from the chart, note down any patterns that indicate your most significant challenges.

Identifying Your Essential Competencies

As you move through this book, you will work to identify the variables impacting your performance as a leader and develop a personalized plan to guide you toward working at the outer limits of your capacity. Please review the following diagram and identify the accompanying competencies in each area to anticipate those areas that you expect will be most pertinent to you. You will use the reproducible "A Comprehensive Planning Document for Maintaining Your Leadership Capacity" (page 162) to assist you in implementing a personalized plan in your professional development in the coming years.

Physical Conditioning: I include exercise in my schedule each week.

5: Always	4: Most of the time	3: Inconsistently	2: Occasionally	1: Never

Environmental Support: I build sources of mental and emotional support into my day.

5: Always	4: Most of the time	3: Inconsistently	2: Occasionally	1: Never

Lifestyle Choices: I plan for and carry out choices that support my physical, mental, and emotional well-being as part of my work.

5: Always	4: Most of the time	3: Inconsistently	2: Occasionally	1: Never

Authentic Reflection: I feel that the reflection in my professional work is both valid and meaningful.

5: Always	4: Most of the time	3: Inconsistently	2: Occasionally	1: Never

Time Management: I can schedule and balance the many tasks that confront me as a school leader. I have established a system for scheduling and communicating.

5: Always	4: Most of the time	3: Inconsistently	2: Occasionally	1: Never

Planning and Preparation: I have a predetermined means of preparing for important elements of my work in advance, and I enter each day with the necessary tools to succeed.

5: Always	4: Most of the time	3: Inconsistently	2: Occasionally	1: Never

Prioritization: My approach to work allows me to reorganize my day to ensure that matters of greatest importance receive priority.

5: Always	4: Most of the time	3: Inconsistently	2: Occasionally	1: Never

Outcomes: Areas of highest importance relative to your personal capacity.

1.

2.

3.

Given the opportunities present in these areas, what are the most significant obstacles that prevent you from exploring them? What steps might you be able to take to remove these obstacles?

CHAPTER 2

LEARNING FROM ELITE ATHLETES

Finding Inspiration in Athlete Training Programs

The beginnings of a different approach are to be found in areas with similar challenges. Why reinvent the wheel when others may have proven solutions to problems like our own? Instead, take a more efficient approach and look to other worlds with comparable challenges to see how they have addressed them successfully.

In this case, the world of competitive sports provides thoughts on a different approach to leadership development. The world of sports is littered with programs promising elite-level conditioning and performance enhancement. Most of these programs are different paths to the same destination—they break down conditioning into specific subskills to focus development on areas of highest potential impact. They consider and address a much wider range of variables that impact the individual performance of an athlete. By expanding athletic performance into a wide range of specific subskills and variables, athletes can increase their overall performance by improving many smaller elements of their sport.

So, what are the similarities to leadership development? Both begin by combining individual performance with the overall function of a group within a structured situation or event. Both are complex processes seemingly grounded in specific behaviors (athletics and physical performance, as well as leadership and behavioral decisions) and yet clearly influenced by nearly all elements of human behavior. Both are cumulative processes with combinations of natural abilities and acquired skills built up over time through experiences and explicit learning. Both are highly personal and specific to the abilities, experiences, and knowledge of each individual. Both apply those skills and attributes to a highly complex process that demands high-speed management of multiple variables. These are just a few of the connections.

As you move through this book, you will examine the different ways in which the principles of athletic development apply to training and preparing school leaders. In some cases, the connections are evident—yet in others, you may have to depart from conventional methods of thinking. However, the concept remains the same: to learn as much as you can about a more comprehensive approach to preparing and sustaining school leaders. Naturally, not all the answers to this complex issue can be found in competitive sports, but you will find many ideas that could benefit your current practice. Ultimately, this book should result in different outcomes and systems of support for each person who reads it, just as every athlete has a different path to their own optimal levels of performance.

The process of preparing for and sustaining people within leadership roles requires distinct approaches, varying by both the individual and the role to which they aspire. Individuals bring different strengths and weaknesses to the process of leading and are shaped by their experiences. Each leader evolves within these variables and becomes a cumulative portrait defined by innate abilities and what they learned.

In a similar way, sports demand specific skill sets based on the game itself and the role that athletes play within the sport. Even an individual sport requires specific areas of strength or knowledge. As athletes progress through various levels of competition, these requirements increase and levels of specialization become more complex. The higher the level, the more specific the expectations for both skills and knowledge of technique or tactic. The equation for all sports is the same: natural ability + physical and mental preparation + experience + tactical and strategic knowledge + conditioning = increased outcomes. Competitive sport brings with it a set of tangible metrics because you can measure speed, strength, performance, skill, and other more specific traits. These metrics become the gauge for measuring athletes' advancement and opportunities over time and the level of competition.

To most people who have participated in athletics, the connections between sports and leadership would seem to be obvious and anecdotal. The value of hard work, perseverance, strategic thinking, and accepting one's role on a team are all mutual ideals, yet they lack the specificity needed to form the basis of a more formal effort to develop either athletes or leaders in a meaningful way. Here, the opportunities are found within the details. To substantiate this connection in an actionable way, the following chapters focus on more specific connections between the worlds of sports and leadership.

This chapter continues that examination by looking at seven traits of preparation for athletic training programs. It continues to explain the value of measuring what matters most as a means of quantifying improvement and performance. It then discusses the merits of a competency-based approach for building leadership capacity to operationalize already-high expectations of leaders' time and effort. Finally, it discusses some strategies for handling public and organizational perceptions of changes that must be made to build leadership capacity.

Exploring the Seven Traits of Athletic Training Programs

For the purposes of this book and the desire to establish personalized and sustainable approaches to leadership development, this book focuses on the following seven traits commonly found in the world of sports. These traits, which you first saw in the introduction (page 1), form the foundation of general practice around preparing athletes for competition. The following provides a closer look at some ways the seven traits of athletic training programs can be applied to leadership development.

1. Managing physiological stress reactions
    - Athletes expect their bodies and minds to react to the stress of their environment in a predictable manner dictated by their body and mind, but they prepare

themselves for that stress activation and manage it in more positive ways in the moment of stress. Stress comes with competition. It cannot be avoided. Therefore, athletes optimize their performance by preparing for that stress instead of trying to lessen it or in some way avoid their natural reactions altogether.

- ¤ For educational leaders, stress is an unavoidable part of our work. What can you do to prepare yourself for it?

2. Addressing physical, mental, emotional, and motivational variables that impact performance levels

- ¤ Athletes acknowledge that, to perform to the outer limits of their abilities, they need to create optimal levels of their own personal readiness. Therefore, they examine all facets of their physical and mental conditioning that can impact performance (even facets that are not traditionally the subject of training and preparation).
- ¤ For educational leaders, consider what variables impact your level of performance in negative ways. What variables form your strengths? What could you do differently to advance your professional practice?

3. Exploring training that is specialized to sport and personalized to athlete

- ¤ Athletes need to remain aware of the specific demands of their sport, event, or position and their own conditioning to work at the outer limits of their potential. They use metrics for performance, a wide variety of parallel training experiences, and supplemental conditioning techniques. Athletes understand the demands of their sport or event, and they are aware of their own state of preparedness relative to those demands.
- ¤ For educational leaders, since you face demands that are specific to your leadership position and circumstances—each of which are addressed by your gifts and talents—how could your ongoing development be more personalized to both?

4. Managing physical, cognitive, and emotional energy

- ¤ Athletes must constantly be aware of the energy required by a situation or event and of their own available energy level. Over-expending energy results in depletion and reduced performance, and under-expending energy means they won't be adequately prepared or performing at their potential during an event. Over-expending is as detrimental as under-expending, which means that accurate monitoring of energy level is crucial for optimal performance.

- For educational leaders, if energy expenditure is a key component to your ongoing capacity, how might you preserve it for more demanding times without sacrificing daily performance? How might you expand the overall amount of energy you bring to work?

5. Using simulation and mental rehearsal

    - By simulating moments of competition that result in elevated emotion or accelerated cognitive processing, athletes can slow down the pace of competition, the emotional complexities of their surroundings, and the myriad decisions that must be made under the duress of a fast-paced environment. This simulation results in diminished anxiety before competition and faster processing and reactions during competition. Athletes use both physical simulation and mental rehearsal or visualization of key moments in competition.

    - For educational leaders, given the positive impact of simulation and rehearsal on overall stress level and performance, what elements of your work lend themselves to the use of these strategies?

6. Maintaining motivational clarity, which is a clear connection between what you are doing and why you are doing it

    - Athletes can sustain themselves in the face of considerable adversity, depleted energy, and pain of all sorts by remaining aware of the factors, values, and experiences that drive them. These foundational ideas become the reasons they persevere. By maintaining awareness of those factors, athletes can sustain their energy and resilience in the face of adversity.

    - For educational leaders, what motivates you? What values form the foundations of your daily decisions? What might you do differently to maintain an active awareness of these values?

7. Using dynamic game planning by planning, planning to adapt, and adapting

- Athletes enter their respective competitions with a plan they believe will allow them to be successful. One hallmark of consistently successful athletes is that they also plan to adapt when confronted with extraneous variables or alternative circumstances. They anticipate circumstances that could necessitate adjustment and include those in their planning before the competition starts. By making as many decisions as possible outside of the pace of competition, athletes give themselves an opportunity to redirect successfully without being influenced by the emotion of a competitive environment. Naturally, it is impossible to prepare for every circumstance, but they can minimize the degree of anxiety they face by preparing for as many as possible. This frees them up to focus on those they had not anticipated.
- For educational leaders, what roles do active planning and adaptation play in your daily work as a leader? Do you plan for contingencies and foreseeable adjustments to those plans?

These seven traits form a framework for considering leadership capacity going forward. Elements of each trait are found within the chapters themselves, and their applications help develop your personalized planning.

In the same manner as in athletic competition, the varying circumstances in school districts result in a wide variety of skills and abilities needed to lead. While they are more difficult to measure and quantify, there are also core aptitudes that any situation requires of those who lead. While leadership skills seem to be a fixed set, they continue to evolve over time as schools and the world become more complicated. The degree to which a leader succeeds over time is reliant on their ability to learn and develop with the changing demands of their environment. This demands an ongoing awareness of the specific leadership skills and strengths to remain current given the demands at hand. However, to make this more comprehensive approach authentic, leaders must be willing to consider their work in the context of smaller and more specific subskills.

As a concrete example of the process of identifying subskills, let's look at the methods athletes use to improve their running speed. Elite athletes work at improving their speed by breaking down the act of running into component parts with each part representing one element of speed. They work at each element separately and then build these components back into the act of running over time (McDonogh, n.d.).

Each of the following components helps an athlete increase their speed.

- **Strength of upper and lower legs:** Fast-twitch muscle fibers generate more acceleration or sustain speed.

- **Core muscular strength:** Leg strength is important, but core muscles (abdominals, lower back, and so on) generate a considerable amount of strength used in running.

- **Running form and efficiency:** There is a solid understanding of the physical movements that create optimal running speed. Athletes learn this and train to replicate this optimal form as they run. They also continue to evaluate their form over time.

- **Stride length and frequency:** Longer strides and more frequent turnover are the very essence of running fast. Athletes must have the flexibility to do both.

- **Endurance and cardiovascular strength:** Different athletic activities require different degrees of endurance. Running fast is only functional if an athlete can maintain that speed over the time required for their sport or event.

- **Mental clarity, motivation, and understanding of form and function:** Elite athletes understand that there is a direct connection between their mental state and their physical performance. For example, pre-competition nerves can result in muscular tension, which creates both fatigue and diminished flexibility. In contrast, a runner can increase their degree of flexibility and blood flow if they can remain relaxed in the moments leading up to competition. The proper mental state supports optimal performance levels, particularly in running fast.

- **Variation of technique based on circumstance and strategy:** Various events or sports have different requirements when it comes to running fast. Some require straight-line speed while others demand lateral quickness or change of direction, meaning there are different values to either short, quick strides or long, smooth ones depending on the requirements of the sport. Each sport requires a different approach to each of the previous components.

There are certainly even more nuanced elements in developing running speed, but these are sufficient to illustrate the degree to which elite athletes are expected to train components of this skill. They learn to break down what seems to be a single, intuitive act (running) into a series of related movements and abilities. This is not to say that every athlete will develop every one of these components. Instead, they come to understand which of these are already strengths of theirs and which hold the greatest promise for impact on their overall performance. Some athletes may benefit from strength training to generate greater acceleration while they run. Others may work to improve their flexibility to increase stride length; others focus on form or techniques that best suit their specific sport or event. In this way, all are working to run faster, though each in different ways.

Leadership development is at least as complex as running fast and, as such, consists of different components that can be understood, evaluated, and developed. Just like the depiction of running, it's possible to identify subcategories of elements that impact your performance within a leadership role.

To complete the comparison, look at the different subskills of effective communication, which is a widely held quality of successful leaders. Each of the following subskills helps a leader communicate more effectively.

- Facility with language in composing a clear and concise message
- Competency in the elements of public speaking, including enunciation, projection, anxiety management, connection with an audience, and so on
- The ability to compose written communication with little or no time
- The ability to maintain a consistent message across various media, audiences, or modes of communication
- Competency with appropriate communications technology
- A comfort level with managing emotionally charged messages during a crisis
- Modulation of both the nature of a message and the way it is delivered for a wide variety of different audiences

Some of these skills are more obvious—and others more obscure—but all are connected to how effectively a leader communicates. All are also observable and developable as independent variables. So, just as it is with a trainer or coach helping an athlete run faster, identifying these elements and how to evaluate each of them helps you build techniques for improving those skills that may be deficient. You can improve your performance by examining it as a function of the sum of its parts.

Measuring What Matters Most

Having oriented your work to the cumulative output of subskills, you arrive at the next challenge, which is to maintain a concrete means of awareness of your status relative to those subskills. You need to be aware of where you stand in a reliable and objective way.

Most are familiar with that irritating yet necessary ritual of an annual physical examination. You visit your doctor's office, knowing that there will be various measurements, and that you will likely be spoken to about at least some of the outcomes. Whether it is body temperature, weight, heart or respiratory rate, blood pressure, or cholesterol numbers, it is a rare achievement to be congratulated by a physician without qualification. So, why would you subject yourself to this experience? Because you know that these variables provide insights into pertinent elements of your physical health. Even if you don't like the results, they tell you something about how your body is performing. There is a direct link between what is measured and your outlook on physical health.

It's the same in schools with educators' work in evaluating students. They think deeply about what they measure in assessments, learn things about what students know and can do, and use that information to guide planning for future work. Educators alter strategies, bring in different resources, adapt practice as needed, offer remediation or enrichment, and build upcoming learning from the information garnered. Yes, at times, there are assessments that are either focused on areas of lower impact or even imposed by outside authorities. These assessments become a part of the overall school program by necessity rather than utility, and you make the best possible use of them. Still, the outcome remains the same—school leaders compile data and use it to guide future learning. What you measure reveals what is important to you. Your values become inherent in your assessments.

The takeaway is that measurement in and of itself is not the outcome. The idea is for data to guide the action you take as a result. You do not go to the doctor's office to try for a personal best blood pressure or cholesterol number. The numbers guide your adjustments to pertinent lifestyle variables. In this way, measurement becomes a much more deliberate process. It shows what you know and can do, and it guides what you need to work on next.

This relates to leader development because it magnifies the importance of what you measure in yourself as a leader and how you measure it. Often, in the crunch of time and priorities, leaders turn to variables that are either readily available or composed from larger series or systems. They turn to sources of data that, while readily available, are often composed of variables thoroughly confounded by extraneous factors well beyond the impact of leadership. Take, for example, the idea of using standardized test scores as a metric for evaluating a leader. Yes, test scores are a measurement of student learning in time. They provide a snapshot of student understanding. But test scores are heavily influenced by extraneous variables, such as environmental conditions, sample sizes, and other challenges well beyond the purview of leaders. Growth targets may be a far more impactful metric to examine in indexing student achievement and school leadership. Therefore, the evaluating organization should measure leadership performance in a manner that is highly mindful, personalized, and specific to the circumstances in which the leader works.

The process of measuring leadership performance begins with determining the organization's expectations of the organization, the community it serves, and ultimately the strengths and weaknesses of the individual leader. From that point, you can compose specific expectations or outcomes that are indexed to the specific needs of a leader or the community they lead. You can measure what matters most and build learning experiences focused on areas of greatest leverage.

If measuring and evaluating leadership performance are such pivotal parts of professional growth, the best approach to the process provides the most useful information while remaining implementable in a realistic manner. After all, the school leader's days and years are already more than full—adding still more to their plates seems like a horrible idea. Therefore, let's turn to what already works well for students, which is authentic performance assessments presented in the context of your existing work.

To facilitate this process, you can use your existing goal-setting and evaluation processes to establish the foundation for your work, which keeps you consistent with existing policies, district-specific evaluation tools, and certification standards. These documents establish a list of job-specific expectations for each leader within their role. From there, you can reflect on those areas of greatest strength and need to prioritize subsequent work. These standards become the focal point of what you will build, with an acknowledgment that areas of strength will be de-emphasized in the immediate-term training and goal setting. De-emphasizing areas of strength frees up additional time and resources to focus attention on other variables, such as physical well-being or cognitive health, that may have a more substantive impact on performance.

One of the best ways for school leaders to implement sustainable approaches for maintaining their leadership capacity is to address it within their current system of professional development, as opposed to implementing it as a separate or new system. The reproducible, "Protocol for Building the Work in the Current System" (page 47), is designed to provide leaders with a starting point for that process.

Considering the Merits of a Competency-Based Approach

The tool kit for an effective approach to personalized professional learning already exists in competency-based learning. Whether your district is among those currently developing a competency-based system for students or not won't restrict you from using that approach for leaders' learning, but it will help to establish a larger framework of what constitutes competency-based learning. You have an opportunity to apply this concept to existing models, resulting in a more targeted form of learning within your existing system.

The competency-based learning model is in different stages of development in the United States and many other countries. The concept is straightforward. Instead of measuring what is learned in units of time, it is measured by the individual learner demonstrating their comprehension. The result is an approach to learning that is far more personalized and efficient. With an emphasis on an ongoing demonstration of their understanding, learners focus their time on what they are ready to learn next. Naturally, the details and operation of a competency-based learning system are far more nuanced than this simple definition, so have a look at the concept in action.

In *Unpacking the Competency-Based Classroom: Equitable, Individualized Learning in a PLC at Work*, Jonathan G. Vander Els and Brian M. Stack (2022) describe an approach to competency-based learning built from a definition of competency-based education called the seven design principles. These design principles, as set forth by the Aurora Institute (Levine & Patrick, 2019), are intended to create a common language for the implementation of competency-based learning in schools.

- **Design principle 1:** Students are empowered daily to make important decisions about their learning experiences, how they will create and apply knowledge, and how they will demonstrate their learning.
- **Design principle 2:** Assessment is a meaningful, positive, and empowering learning experience for students that yields timely, relevant, and actionable evidence.
- **Design principle 3:** Students receive timely, differentiated support based on their individual learning needs.
- **Design principle 4:** Students progress based on evidence of mastery not seat time.
- **Design principle 5:** Students learn actively using different pathways and varied pacing.
- **Design principle 6:** Strategies to ensure equity for all students are embedded in the culture, structure, and pedagogy of schools and education systems.
- **Design principle 7:** Rigorous, common expectations for learning (knowledge, skills, and dispositions) are explicit, transparent, measurable, and transferable.

With the wide variety of approaches to competency-based learning across the profession, this definition allows for common language and goals as the work progresses. The intent of competency-based learning remains consistent—focus learning on what individuals are ready to learn. While a time-based system works for a narrow band of learners, many either are ready to progress faster or require additional resources for support or remediation. The concept of learning by competency remains one of the most significant shifts in the approach to formal learning. It has taken on a variety of different forms in working with students, yet it remains largely untapped as a resource for professional development.

This is particularly true for leaders, who tend to consider their own professional learning as an afterthought, just behind both the learning of students and teachers. They tend to give themselves the time and resources left over after everyone else is cared for. Understandably, this means time and resources are thin for their own learning. Why not adopt a model that is more personalized and focuses on the material you are most in need of learning?

As you look to leverage the concept of competency-based learning for leaders, you can apply these seven design principles (Levine & Patrick, 2019) to the task of leadership development as follows.

1. Leaders are empowered daily to make decisions about their learning experiences. One key element to leadership is the leader assumes responsibility for their own learning, independent of requirements.

    - For example, most districts include programming for all leaders in their professional learning standard. What if you were to build in elements of choice within that programming, as well as the potential for leaders to design their own learning experiences?

2. Assessment is a meaningful, positive, and empowering experience for leaders. The more accurate and job-embedded the assessment tasks, the greater the degree of personalization for what should be learned next.

    - For example, rather than building out assessment tasks that live outside of the leader's daily responsibilities (such as additional readings, reflections, or activities), consider an approach that uses job-embedded activities as means of demonstrating competency (evidence of a functioning community engagement effort as opposed to a manufactured plan do accomplish the same).

3. Leaders receive timely, differentiated support. Specific interventions result in specific outcomes.

    - For example, struggling leaders receive support in reactive fashion through improvement plans or directives generally following a negative evaluation. What if that support were to be proactively built in for administrators in the form of coaching or a facilitated support network as dictated by their level of experience? (Leaders who are new to the profession receive more intensive support, leaders new to the district receive less structured but present support, and veteran leaders receive directed support.)

4. Leaders' progress is based on evidence of mastery, not seat time. Time is among the rarest and most-valued resources for those with full schedules. This component ensures that available time is spent learning material that can produce the highest degree of result.

- For example, as mentioned previously, a leader's individual learning is determined by their areas of greatest opportunity instead of a broad spectrum of nonspecific support. They don't do the whole checklist. They just focus on the areas of highest leverage.

5. Leaders learn actively using different pathways and varied pacing. School leaders' responsibilities vary widely. In addition, leaders' gifts and talents bring different things to that work. Various communities expect different things from leaders. Learning is standardized for the convenience of the system producing the learning, not for those in need of it. Building elements of differentiation supports the development of each individual leader within the confines of the work they do.

    - For example, much of professional learning is delivered under a time crunch, and there is often little attention given to individual leaders' learning styles, aptitudes, or challenges. What if you applied the same sense of differentiation to leaders that you know is effective with students? Multimodal delivery methods, varied pacing, and situationally responsive content all will work as well for leaders as they do for students.

6. Strategies to ensure equity for all leaders are embedded in the culture, structure, and pedagogy of schools and education systems. All leaders are different and do different work to advance student learning. While that work demands personalization, it must always be conducted with an eye for equitable support and opportunity.

    - For example, while standards are useful in establishing learning progressions, educators in all roles must develop instructional experiences that are responsive to the needs of their community, to the resources at their disposal, and to the requirements of the learners in their charge. The same should be expected from leaders. Leaders in rural communities have different needs than those in urban environments, and larger schools have different challenges than smaller schools. The opportunity arises when you place the personal skills and aptitudes of each leader in their environment and build learning around them according to their needs.

7. Rigorous common expectations for learning (knowledge, skills, and dispositions) are explicit, transparent, measurable, and transferable. Competency-based learning is a different approach to acquisition of skill and knowledge. It is not a process of diminished expectations. All learners can advance further than they might have in a more inherently standardized system if the material is presented differently.

    - For example, shifting the focus of time and effort to the areas of greatest opportunity does not weaken the expectation of leaders' learning. Instead, you are targeting areas in their learning that will produce the greatest effect and propel them to work at the outer limits of their abilities.

When phrased as elements of a professional learning system, each principle makes as much sense for leaders as for students. As you construct an approach to professional learning that addresses broader variables and goals, it only makes sense to deploy an approach that recognizes demonstrated learning, focusing valuable time and resources on what each leader is ready to learn and what they need to learn.

While you work on your new approach to professional learning, you must remember that the benefit must be worth the energy expended. Creating anything new requires expending energy, which most school leaders need to conserve. For this reason, it would be inefficient to completely redesign the existing models for professional learning that are functioning effectively. Instead, the following would be valuable uses of time and energy relative to professional learning for leaders.

- A deep examination of the breadth of variables that impact leadership performance beyond the scope of job-specific knowledge and skills
- An acknowledgment of skills and knowledge an individual leader already demonstrates, resulting in that leader's ability to focus on other areas in a more substantive manner
- An element of the evaluation process that facilitates authentic and substantive reflection on a leader's own performance expectations
- A streamlined approach to managing an evaluation process that focuses valuable time and attention on the act of professional learning instead of the administration of professional learning

By building a new approach from what already works, you can create a competency-based approach to personalized professional learning. The next section will discuss how to deal with other peoples' perceptions of this new approach.

Handling Public and Organizational Perception

Educational leaders must deal with the impact of perception on two fundamental levels: (1) the perception of those they lead and (2) that of the constituents they serve. What people think of you, particularly within those two circles, has a direct impact on your capacity to lead.

The perception of those you lead speaks directly to your credibility and ability to guide the organization. The people within your organization cannot be forced to follow you, though you may wish it so. This is particularly true in schools where direct supervision of staff is often a matter of triage rather than comprehensive oversight. School staff follow leaders they respect and those who articulate and advance a vision of teaching and learning consistent with the values of the community they serve. Now, consider the matter of leadership capacity.

If a leader communicates and conveys a value for wellness and professional capacity within the community and that value is consistent for all members, then the practices will be supported and implemented. If a leader advances their own efforts to prioritize professional capacity but does not promote the same within the community, they risk being perceived as hypocritical. The price paid would be credibility and respect, leading to a diminished capacity to lead. Therefore, in remaining consistent with the theme of maximizing leadership capacity, advancing the prioritization of wellness becomes an element of maintaining capacity itself. If those you lead perceive this effort as being exclusive to leadership, you compromise the very point.

As is the case with most staff communication, your actions are often clearer than what you say, although both approaches are worthy of your attention. By advancing time and material for employee wellness initiatives through your human resources programs, you indicate they have value. You can continue the effort by regularly revisiting these programs in faculty meetings and newsletters, endorsing participation, and promoting specific events. You build value by both direct communication and active participation on an ongoing basis. By establishing a broader value for wellness across your school or district, you contextualize your own participation along with those you lead.

Therefore, your words and actions also communicate a systemwide prioritization of capacity to your wider communities. Beginning with policymakers (school boards, school committees, and so on) and extending to parents and community, taking time to communicate the reasons behind these efforts forms a foundation for the acceptance of personal well-being for leaders and staff.

It's essential to remain sensitive to how people perceive the new wellness efforts; this allows you to counter potential misperceptions that your emphasis on wellness somehow indicates a lesser commitment to the work. This is an age of high expectations for school leaders to remain accessible at all hours or to respond to communication in a matter of minutes. It is difficult enough for leaders to prioritize sleep, exercise, and schedule demands without this added pressure. You can carve out time, given the conventions of reasonable work hours and accessibility, so long as there is a broader understanding of your commitment to capacity. There are, of course, reasonable boundaries. In an extreme example, why invite unneeded scrutiny by spending two hours at the gym midday? (Obviously, common sense should prevail.) More commonly, your presence at evening events or cocurricular functions provides a sound illustration. If you establish a rotation for coverage of evening events to prioritize family time and schedule exercise before or after school hours, you send a message to everyone about the priority of this time. Better yet, when you communicate these schedules, you present an opportunity for community awareness of your intent. Not all community members will find this compelling, but understanding the schedule provides clarity to members who want to understand what school leaders do. Communicating the value of balance and establishing it in a clear way will help form the basis of public perception.

You may not be able to control what people think of you—either within your organization or around it—but by articulating a clear objective for your efforts and applying them consistently to all community members, you form the basis for public perception that will support your work. They may not agree with what you are doing, but if they understand it, you maintain the foundation of trust that will support the work and maintain your capacity to lead.

The following chapters take a closer look at the different factors that impact your health, mental clarity, emotional balance, and motivational foundations, each from the perspective of how they impact your capacity to function in a leadership role. These elements form the framework on which you can build a new, more comprehensive, and more sustainable means of developing practicing leaders and welcoming new leaders into the role.

Questions for Reflection

Use the following questions to help you reflect on what you have read in this chapter.

1. In your current professional learning plan, how much time is committed to developing new knowledge versus revisiting things that are already familiar?

2. What approaches do you employ to measure your professional learning? Do these approaches allow you to focus greater attention on things you need to learn?

3. Based on any experiences you may have as either an athlete, a coach, or a fan of a sport, what training concepts or practices would you like to implement as a leader that would expand your capacity?

4. How much of a concern do you have for potential negative perceptions of wellness efforts by your colleagues, constituents, or community? If this is a concern for you, what steps might you take to inform them? If it is not, how might you use this acceptance to broaden support?

5. Think about your own learning preferences. How many of your professional development activities are directed at those preferences? What experiences might you pursue that are more in line with who you are as a learner?

Protocol for Building the Work in the Current System

Much of chapter 2 is dedicated to the ways you can be more efficient in connecting a broader consideration of pertinent variables to your existing professional development system, whatever that system may be. This allows you to minimize both the disruption of implementing this approach and the time it can take to bring it into practice.

But how can a school district best approach this challenge? The following are a few steps that can be used to increase focus while maintaining current systems.

1. Clarify the expectations of leaders in your district. Whether through standards, performance expectations, or evaluation tools, all districts have some form of articulating what they ask of their leaders.
    - Where are yours located?
    - How are they present in your daily work?
    - How are they demonstrated or evaluated?

2. Evaluate and prioritize the different expectations. Among the expectations that you identified in the previous exercise, is there a way to "weight" these expectations? Are some emphasized over others?
    - District priorities and community expectations are often reflected in what is expected of leaders. What is most important in your community?
    - If some expectations are prioritized, does that mean that others are de-emphasized? If so, does this mean that they may be either eliminated or demonstrated in other ways beyond conventional evaluation methods?
    - Can some expectations be combined with one another or integrated with variables impacting wellness and capacity?

3. Discern the difference between commonly held expectations and those that hold specific pertinence to a given role.
    - For example, "In our district, *all* leaders are expected to _____, regardless of their position or assignment."
    - There are differences between leading an elementary school versus a high school and building leadership versus systems leadership. Are these differences articulated anywhere in your

current system? If so, how might these differences be reflected in the expression of variables impacting wellness and capacity? If not, are there opportunities to add these differentiations?

4. Examine your current system for opportunities to track and evaluate elements of physical, cognitive, emotional, and motivational well-being. Are there existing tenets of your system that accommodate these priorities?

- Elements of professional development plans, such as action research, the ability to organize and add activities, or even human resources–sponsored wellness initiatives, all provide a context for integrating capacity-building work in a way that is both measurable and consistent.

- Does your current system allow for modifying existing district goals, wellness initiatives, or priorities? If so, can capacity-building work be integrated into your district in that way?

5. How does your current system accommodate goal setting and authentic reflection? While much of this process involves integrating capacity-building activities in a way that allows for measurement and endorsement at the building or systems level, the option exists to do so as an individual (or group of individuals).

- A system that allows for personalized professional learning goals lends itself naturally to capacity building. Chart your own path.

- Separate from formalized methods of recognizing and measuring professional development, activities that result in increased capacity are simply a healthy, beneficial choice! Are you willing to engage in capacity building without receiving credit from your formal professional development system?

CHAPTER 3

MANAGING STRESS REACTIONS

Stress and the Four-Foot Putt

The key factor, in both sports and educational leadership, rests in developing a fundamental understanding of what stress does to your body. As you come to understand these natural biological reactions, you are better able to recognize stress responses when they occur and respond accordingly. The process of channeling your stress response into something that is more beneficial and healthier requires an intentional approach before, during, and after an event.

In competitive athletics, stress can be an asset and a liability. The activation of the stress response provides additional blood flow, oxygen, and glucose to muscle tissues, rendering them more energized than they are at rest. On the other hand, the narrowed visual field and physiological tension that result hinder performance (American Psychological Association, 2018). To limit the stress of competition to a beneficial impact, athletes must learn to channel the positive elements while minimizing the negative outcomes. For some athletes, this happens with little conscious effort. Others are never able to accomplish it. For those who don't, the pressure will ultimately be the factor that limits their opportunities to rise within the levels of competition.

Let's look at a quintessential example of a stressful moment: the four-foot putt to win a golf tournament. The ball is so close to the hole that it seems like a given that the player will make the shot under any circumstances, particularly if the player has elite skills. Just a little tap, and the ball will roll into the hole. So, why is this putt so daunting?

It is because the outcomes are so significant. Make the shot and win. The years of preparation to compete all come down to this one simple act. If ever there were a moment of psychologically induced stress reaction, this is it. The golfer's own brain has concocted a full range of reactions. Their only chance to execute the shot in a routine way is to overcome these reactions. The golfer must approach the shot like any other. They must slow the sympathetic reaction's cascade and remember their training and preparation. The golfer breathes deep, relaxes, and moves back the putter, guided by muscle motor memory.

As leaders gain experience and time in their roles, they realize that stress is simply a part of the work. Any thoughts of making the job less stressful ignore the weight of the work. Therefore, this chapter will look at what biological stress reactions do to the body and mind, and how you can frame stress in different ways as you strive to work at the outer limits of your potential.

Stressful events and how you interact with them make up the most prominent element of leaders' internal challenges. It also represents the most significant drain on your overall capacity to function. Your stress response impacts nearly all elements of your well-being and functioning. In moments of perceived stress, your brain "[is] designed to protect your body in an emergency by preparing you to react quickly" (Pietrangelo, 2023). Plotting a productive path toward optimal levels of performance under these adaptations begins with a clear understanding of what stress is and what it does to you, for better or worse.

An athlete must channel the positive elements of their escalated stress response without allowing it to spill over to a point where the physiological changes begin to limit their performance. For example, the addition of available oxygen and glucose brought about by a cortisol surge provides valuable fuel to an athlete's muscles. However, if those muscles become engaged to a point where their tension begins to constrict blood flow, the positive becomes a negative (American Psychological Association, 2018). Muscle tension results in decreased flexibility and muscle memory, as well as possible cramping or limited reaction time. This is the origin of the term *choking*, which is common vernacular regarding athletes who find themselves unable to perform under pressure. The solution? Athletes prepare themselves to perform physically and mentally so they become more relaxed when they are in pressure-packed situations. They train themselves to slow down intentional cognitive processing and trust in the conditioning they've worked so hard to develop.

As a leader, you can channel that same approach to your own stress reactions. By developing a fundamental understanding of how your body reacts to stress, you can prepare yourself to engage physically and cognitively in those moments. You can use the stress of a given situation to provide additional fuel to sustain yourself instead of giving in to physiological responses and potential negative outcomes. It all starts by understanding how your body is designed to work in stressful situations.

This chapter begins by explaining what stress is and why it is necessary. Then, it discusses the fight-or-flight response to perceived threats and the strain it causes on the body. Next, it delves into the effect of longer-term stressors before examining exactly what makes something threatening and explores stress's connection to health and illness. Finally, it talks about a few things to keep in mind that can help reduce stress.

Everyone sees the nature and degree of stress in their own ways. What may be a horrible experience for one person may be engaging for another. As such, it's important for you to know how you view the different elements of school leadership relative to how they impact you. The reproducible, "Understanding the Context of Your Stress Reactions" (page 63), is designed to facilitate your reflection on which parts of your work are engaging and which fill you with degrees of dread.

Understanding Stress Reactions

This exploration of stress reactions begins with the concept of arousal. In the American Psychological Association dictionary of psychological terms, *arousal* (2018) is defined as "a state of physiological activation or cortical responsiveness, associated with sensory stimulation and activation of fibers from the reticular activating system." In other words, it's something that catches your attention. An incident must produce some kind of arousal for it to catch your interest. In the positive sense, events that are perceived as stressful to any degree capture attention. You lock in on the situation and engage more fully. Problems arise as the event escalates, and you begin to perceive your situation as a potential source of danger. Your physical responses continue to transform, and your body chemistry changes dramatically in anticipation of what is to come.

Everyone sees situations through their own lenses and reacts accordingly to how they interpret those situations. Danger to one person is fun to another. The relative nature of your experiences is why these reactions can more accurately be characterized as arousal.

Robert M. Yerkes and John D. Dodson (1908) were among the earliest researchers to explore relativity of arousal in their research. Their work, now foundational in the academic fields of psychology, is known as *Yerkes-Dodson Law*, which illustrates the relationship between levels of arousal and levels of performance in a bell curve (Nickerson, 2023) shown in figure 3.1. The takeaway from their work, which is still pertinent today, is that levels of performance are reliant on the presence of at least some arousal. Too little arousal means no interest and no performance. Too much arousal means performance falls off quickly.

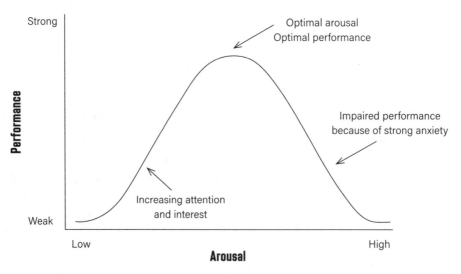

Source: *Diamond, Campbell, Park, Halonen, & Zoladz, 2007, licensed under CC BY 3.0 (https:// creativecommons.org/licenses/by/3.0).*

FIGURE 3.1: Yerkes-Dodson's relationship between arousal and performance.

Given the Yerkes-Dodson Law, it is safe to say that you rely on some form of stress even to engage in your daily work. The curve begins to bend upward when a situation piques your interest. In other words, you care about what's happening. As the situation becomes more complex, your level of performance gradually rises until you reach the peak level of your performance. Then, arousal becomes overwhelming as you find yourself outside of your capacity to engage it. Anxiety takes hold. At that point, your performance levels begin to dip sharply. The negative impacts are easily recognizable as what is typically considered as stress. In all, the curve in figure 3.1 depicts a balance between engagement and anxiety. An ideal situation must present you with enough challenge to be engaging, with the given risk that—at some point as arousal rises—it could become stressful.

Understanding Fight or Flight

We begin to think of a situation as dangerous as risk accumulates. That's when the sympathetic nervous system kicks in, and it "functions like a gas pedal in a car" (Harvard Health Publishing, 2024). It triggers the fight-or-flight response, which is your body's natural reaction to some form of challenge or perceived threat. Your body is designed to respond with a series of different accommodations, primarily through hormones and neurochemicals such as dopamine, epinephrine, and cortisol, which seems to have become the ultimate villain of human biochemistry. The chemical cocktail that your body produces gives you greater strength, thinking power, energy, and attention in times when you need it (Fabritius & Hagemann, 2017). Naturally, there is a price for these reactions.

Difficulties arise when either this response is activated more frequently than your body can handle or the response remains activated for prolonged periods of time (Guidi, Lucente, Sonino, & Fava, 2020). The wonderfully adaptive nature of your body can then work against you because it will adapt to these conditions as well. The strain resulting from this adaptation is referred to as *allostatic load*, which is defined as "the cost of chronic exposure to fluctuating or heightened neural and neuroendocrine responses resulting from repeated or chronic environmental challenges that an individual reacts to as being particularly stressful" (Guidi et al., 2020, p. 11). In other words, allostatic load is the strain placed on your body's physical systems by prolonged or frequent responses to stress.

Your recognition of a stressful situation begins with the release of the previously mentioned chemical cocktail into your bloodstream. The brain's call for more fuel brings an elevated heart rate to deliver more oxygen to the brain and the muscles, but also brings increased blood pressure and strain on the circulatory system (American Psychological Association, 2018). Your brain and muscles get the oxygen they need but at a cost. Cortisol release also frees up stored glucose to give your muscles more energy, though it won't take that glucose from fat stores. Energy storage is out of business at that moment, so the body goes to muscle tissue and the liver to find the glucose it needs. They are both still functioning. Your body will also shut down the immune system, the digestive system, and the reproductive system to focus resources on the brain and body in response to the stressor (Pietrangelo, 2023). It's not tough to imagine how the prolonged absence of each of these systems can bring about negative results. In the end, your body has transformed itself into a more efficient fighting or fleeing machine, but it has placed a great deal of strain (allostatic load) on other important body systems in doing so (Burn, 2020; Sapolsky, 2004).

Looking at Longer-Term Stressors

In most cases, allostatic load and the related negative stress outcomes aren't a result of a single stress response but instead come from either repeated or prolonged exposure to perceived stressors. A fundamentally healthy body can handle short episodes of this strain, but the longer or more frequent it becomes, the more wear and tear. Your body will respond to a perceived stressor, whether it is physiologically conditioned to handle the strain or not. If you are living with diminished capacity in one (or several) of your bodily systems due to health conditions, the impact of increased allostatic load will show up in the affected systems (Burn, 2020). Some causes of these compromised body systems are within your control and others are not (Burn, 2020).

By developing awareness of the significant ways in which allostatic load manifests in your daily life, you can counteract it. For this reason, any effort to establish a comprehensive approach to maintaining your professional capacity will be dependent on accurate and specific data regarding your current health. You must know what works well and what doesn't, what you can do to affect any deficiencies, and how those reactions should be prioritized.

Now, take a closer look at the concept of allostatic load to understand why job stress leaves you feeling so depleted. As a complex biological system, your body always seeks out the most efficient or balanced state of functioning, usually in the interest of preserving valuable energy. This point of functioning becomes a healthy baseline (homeostasis or stable state of equilibrium) for all the systems in your body. The measurement of these baselines indicates the status of your overall health. Your body will adapt to the circumstances and conditions that you encounter each day in the ways it deems most necessary and beneficial for continued efficient operation. The resulting energy needed to respond physiologically (and otherwise) places demands on your body's systems, the degree of which is based on the variation needed from your baseline (Guidi et al., 2020). Your body adapts to these demands, establishing a new set of conditions—a new baseline, which is generally different from what would be your preferred state. This new baseline is called a state of *allostasis* (n.d.) or maintaining equilibrium "in response to actual or perceived environmental and psychological stressors." Your body is still looking for balance, but this time in a manner that accommodates the demands placed on it by your external or internal environment. The resulting strain on your body, mind, and so on is how you arrive at allostatic load (McEwen, 2000).

Consider blood pressure, which is a common indicator of health. The pressure at which blood flows changes by variations and adaptations in the heartbeats, which usually are brought on by some form of demand for extra oxygen somewhere in the body. This demand can be a result of physical exertion, the condition of the circulatory system, injury, immune response, or activation of the stress response. A call goes out for more blood (and with it, oxygen and glucose), and the heart responds by beating harder and faster (American Psychological Association, 2018). Sometimes this is a short-term response or an ongoing and eventually chronic situation. The increase in pressure puts strain on the heart and blood vessels, which are operating above their ideal homeostatic levels (Harvard Health Publishing, 2024; Sapolsky, 2004). Just like the plumbing in a house, if the pump is working too hard and the pipes are under pressure, eventually, the pipes could wear down, clog, or leak. The vascular system has similar qualities.

While blood pressure is certainly a prominent component of allostatic load, it is just one component. There are many more elements that are part of the body's efforts to maintain its level of functioning, ranging from the physical (pulse, optical focus, and muscle tension) to the cognitive (memory transfer, sleep patterns, and so on) to the emotional (rumination, focus, and so on; American Psychological Association, 2018; Sapolsky, 2004). These elements will form the focus of some of the upcoming chapters.

Examining What Makes Something Threatening

So, what gets the whole stress ball rolling? It starts with what you see as a threat. You have the run-of-the-mill immediate physical threat, which is generally characterized in some literature as a bear or a tiger. Anything that can eat you will do. Your perception of the danger is a given, and this hypothetical predator looks hungry. The brain sees the danger and signals the autonomic nervous system to begin the sympathetic response. Your body is ready to fight or flee.

Next are perceived threats. The human brain has evolved into an amazing connection-making system. Not only can it recognize threats in the present, but it can also relive and remember those in the past and predict those that have not happened yet (Kramer et al., 2022). That's where things get interesting because this includes the ability to, without your conscious permission, initiate a sympathetic response to those threats. Unfortunately, bodies and minds are designed to react in the same way whether a threat is standing in front of you or painted in detail in your imaginations (Kramer et al., 2022). For example, those in stressful district- or school-leadership jobs may awaken periodically during the night. Let's say that you try to go back to sleep when you remember that you have a nine o'clock budget meeting in the morning. The following thought process unfolds.

You need to add funds to your building operations lines because you forgot to factor in a contractual increase. You need to call your supplier before the meeting to verify costs. You also need to meet with your facilities manager to factor in potential overruns or complications. Hanrahan will be at the meeting. That arrogant know-it-all loves to catch you on every detail. What makes him so special? The guy is just so obnoxious and difficult. It's like he enjoys antagonizing you. Remember when he called you out on your supply increases last year in a public school board meeting? He was so smug.

Let the activation begin.

It doesn't matter that you're in bed trying to sleep or that the alarm will ring soon. Your heart is racing, blood pressure elevates, and epinephrine and cortisol flow. You're ready to do battle with Hanrahan at two o'clock in the morning. So much for sleep.

There are no off switches to the analytical or predictive functions of your mind. Instead of being wired to respond to dangers you see in front of you, your mind synthesizes the memories that you have stored away with predictive elements of your surroundings to produce a whole volume of different potential threats that trigger arousal. Once your mind goes down those roads, your body will follow in the ways it is designed.

It's simple to say that you shouldn't let your brain roam like that or let Hanrahan get under your skin to that degree. During times when natural processes interfere with healthy ones, it is less a matter of what should happen and more of what you do about it.

While everyone perceives stress levels differently, we also find opportunities for a healthy response to that stress. The reproducible, "A Path to Mindfulness, Authentic Reflection, and Self-Awareness" (page 68), is designed to guide you through a simple, introductory experience of mindful relaxation.

Exploring Stress's Connection to Health and Illness

Most know intuitively that stressful experiences leave you feeling sick, whether from the effects of cortisol deactivating the digestive tract, the increase of blood flow to your head, or the effect the cocktail of associated stress hormones has on your whole body. You just feel sick—and for good reason. The sympathetic nervous system is disruptive to what is considered normal functioning of major bodily systems (Harvard Health Publishing, 2024). It stands to reason that you would feel out of sorts at the very least. What about actual illnesses, though? Do frequent or prolonged stress responses bring about greater probability of illnesses? Yes, they do (Sapolsky, 2004).

The more frequently these stress activations occur, the more time the body is susceptible to illness (Yaribeygi, Panahi, Sahraei, Johnston, & Sahebkar, 2017). The greater the impact of allostasis, the more diminished you find your ability to fight off and heal from infections or disease. Were it just these two factors, you could make sense of this risk and prepare for it. However, the issue is more serious. According to the American Psychological Association (2013), chronic exposure to a stress response has a much broader reach relative to your physical health:

> The long-term activation of the stress response system and the overexposure to cortisol and other stress hormones that come with it can disrupt almost all of your body's processes. This can put you at increased risk for a variety of physical and mental health problems, including anxiety, depression, digestive issues, headaches, muscle tension and pain, heart disease, heart attack, high blood pressure, stroke, sleep problems, weight gain, and memory and concentration impairment.

While this paints a fairly comprehensive picture of how stress may affect your health, evidence of a longer-term impact exists. The health issues cited in the quotation also bring a cumulative impact over time and can cause subsequent chronic health issues to emerge or worsen. Long-term exposure to stress without some form of proactive preparation for the body will lead to significant health issues (Yaribeygi et al., 2017).

Earlier, this chapter discussed the fascinating way that bodies can initiate a sympathetic nervous system response simply by thinking about a threat, whether from memories of the past or in anticipation of the future. This connects the physiological elements of the stress reaction with events that are in the past, or in an imagined version of the future, and explains how perceived stress can impact how the body functions. Therefore, worry can impact your health.

Many health care providers and credible online resources provide strategies for managing anxiety and the physiological impact of stress. Common threads through many of these resources include physical activity, healthy sleep, and avoiding drugs and alcohol. These healthy living tips are also found throughout the literature on optimal functioning (Cleveland Clinic, n.d.; Mayo Clinic Staff, 2023a). Most of these resources also advocate widely held practices for reducing the impact of a stressful situation, many of which will be addressed in chapter 6 (page 103). All these resources include two common themes: (1) the importance of general health and (2) intentionally addressing the source of anxiety.

Although most leaders know there are resources that can help them navigate the physiological elements of stress, few use them. As previously discussed, leaders do not necessarily prioritize their physical health, and even fewer consider it to be a key component of professional capacity. Leaders push through the fallout of work, intent on seeing responsibilities through in the interest of students and staff. Unfortunately, stress and anxiety can make them physically sick. Ignoring that outcome or attempting to push through it without some form of attention only worsens the impact, disrupting optimal performance.

With the commonality of the biochemical and physical responses to stress, there are a few physical factors that leaders can employ to prepare their bodies for long-term or repetitive exposure to a sympathetic response. Rather than focus solely on the activities and outcomes, turn instead to the resulting physical conditions that increase the likelihood of sustaining optimum health under stress. While some of these factors are consistent with conventional fitness programs, the intended focus is on cardiovascular and metabolic resilience. Most of the body's responses to elevated arousal involve an exaggerated reaction by the circulatory system. Your body believes that it is necessary to divert blood to the mind and muscles and away from tasks such as digestion. This provides needed glucose and oxygen to the areas where the body feels they are most needed, placing strain on the heart and increasing blood pressure, resulting in a decrease in digestion's effectiveness (American Psychological Association, 2018; Sapolsky, 2004). The following list breaks down cardiovascular and digestive health.

- **Cardiovascular health:** Because of the specific impact stress hormones have on the circulatory system, physical preparation of this specific bodily function must be a priority to maintain leadership capacity. The stress response tests the strength and resilience of your heart and circulatory system and can introduce health complications very quickly if required to operate beyond capacity. Therefore, both cardiovascular exercise and a heart-healthy diet are central to maintaining leadership capacity (Chu, Marwaha, Sanvictores, Awosika, & Ayers, 2024).
    - ¤ Are you aware of the components of a heart-healthy diet and cardiovascular exercise? Do you regularly include both in your lifestyle? If not, this would make an appropriate focus for a goal.
- **Digestive health:** Although digestive health is not normally something that attracts attention in a physical fitness program, the diversion of oxygen and glucose from the digestive system results in outcomes that can detract from healthy bodily functions, the reception of necessary nutrients the body needs to stay healthy, and distracting physical symptoms that decrease a person's ability to respond to the demands of in-the-moment leadership functions. Effective metabolic functioning relies on a balance of gut bacteria, which can be upset quickly by the body's arousal. There are also time constraints and neurological connections to digestion under stress that can result in complications within the digestive tract. You could experience a range of maladies from simple indigestion to far more complex disorders, such as irritable bowel syndrome or Crohn's disease. These complications can manifest themselves as mere short-term inconveniences, but when prolonged can be a considerable drain on the level of personal wellness needed to sustain capacity under stress (Chu et al., 2024; Sapolsky, 2004).
    - ¤ Are you aware of the foundations of digestive health? Do you incorporate dietary choices that support a healthy digestive system? The nutrition that powers your body

enters through this system; without a healthy functioning gut biome, your body will not have the building blocks it needs to sustain you through the challenges of your work. A basic understanding of digestive functioning and nutrition can bring significant improvements to your overall health and physical resilience.

While this book is arranged into sections to develop a picture showing the different components of capacity in a concrete manner, there are certainly ways in which your physical, cognitive, and emotional functions intersect. Your stress reaction is one of them. One key element of this concept is taking active steps to slow your mind while you attend to your body. The mind and body are connected neurologically—it becomes important for you to take steps to slow your thoughts just as much as to slow your heart rate or breathing.

One of the more widely recognized approaches to slowing your thoughts is a technique known as mindfulness. The American Psychological Association (n.d.) defines *mindfulness* as an "awareness of one's internal states and surroundings. Mindfulness can help people avoid destructive or automatic habits and responses by learning to observe their thoughts, emotions, and other present-moment experiences without judging or reacting to them." In other words, shifting your awareness and attention to the internal workings of your body can gain you control over how you react to external circumstances. By establishing a greater internal awareness of how your body functions, you can purposefully impact the physiological components of your stress reaction. Building a meaningful and substantive plan for managing your stress reaction begins with understanding what stress does to you personally and what strategies are most meaningful and effective. As a reminder, you can explore mindfulness in the reproducible, "A Path to Mindfulness, Authentic Reflection, and Self-Awareness" (page 68).

The hypothetical two o'clock in the morning fight with Hanrahan (page 56) is a product of a complicated interaction between biology, psychology, and autonomic processes resulting from a very long evolutionary process. Your body thinks it is protecting itself. By recognizing your response as such, you allow yourself to create counter narratives to the perception and take proactive steps to de-escalate the initial response. Your conscious mind remains your most effective means of responding (Huberman, 2021).

Therefore, educational leaders can acknowledge that their work is stressful and that different leaders will find different things more stressful than others. Each person is unique in their physical capacity to handle the resulting allostatic load that is part of the work. The opportunities for arousal are inherent in what leaders do. You do not necessarily seek to eliminate the autonomic responses or the brain functions that cause these stress responses. You just look for ways to continue to be healthy and efficient in their presence.

So, where should you begin seeking out actionable strategies for managing your own personal stress response? It starts with an authentic process of self-understanding. If each person takes the time to recognize what they consider stressful and how their bodies and minds react, they can find appropriate ways to anticipate these reactions and to counteract the effects. For example, a person who tends to internalize stress might find themselves susceptible to stress eating or consuming alcohol to reduce their anxiety. By realizing that, the individual can anticipate that reaction and plan for it by purchasing healthier foods or planning exercise as a de-escalation technique rather than a bottle of wine. While this approach sounds like an oversimplification, it illustrates how understanding the stress response and a measure of self-awareness can produce actionable strategies for making healthier choices.

The following chapters will dive deeply into different ways in which autonomic stress responses can impact physical, cognitive, and emotional well-being. Armed with that understanding, you can reflect further on how this example illustrates your own personal stress reaction. While the resulting techniques vary from the obvious to the discreet, none are easy to implement without awareness and understanding. The reproducible, "Capacity Overview Graphic Organizer" (page 70), can help you gain a more comprehensive context for leadership capacity as it will be explored in upcoming chapters.

Questions for Reflection

Use the following questions to help you reflect on what you have read in this chapter.

1. What physical or cognitive changes do you recognize in yourself when you become stressed? How do you think those changes impact your job performance?
2. Under what situations does stress enhance your performance?
3. Have you ever experienced health concerns or challenges because of a stressful situation? If so, what advice have you received from your health care provider to mitigate that concern? If not, what strategies

might you prepare for if you do experience stress-related health challenges?

4. Where might you turn to for advice or guidance regarding how best to handle a challenging or complex issue within the context of your work?

5. What strategies does your school or district use to prepare you for stressful situations? What resources are available to you for support during or following these situations?

Understanding the Context of Your Stress Reactions

Everyone encounters stressful events in different ways; what is considered stressful can vary from person to person. Stress can also either hinder or elevate performance, depending on your perspective. Stress may help you focus and energize you, or it may cause you to freeze or act out of frustration. In the chart that follows, please find a list of events that can occur in schools during a typical day. Use the scale to indicate the degree to which these types of events either energize you or limit your performance during such situations. Your final responses will help you identify areas of responsibility where you can focus subsequent learning or professional development.

Remember that your challenge is not to solve these issues but to identify the way you experience the stressor. Will it enhance your performance or hamper it?

Academic Challenges					
Concentration	Dread	Discomfort	Indifference	Engaged	Energized
You receive a call from a parent challenging their child's final term grade.	1	2	3	4	5
A student raises an objection to the validity or viability of a book assigned by their teacher.	1	2	3	4	5
A student in your school demonstrates a level of skill and knowledge beyond your existing mathematics program. The parents request to meet with you to discuss alternatives.	1	2	3	4	5
In examining your assessment scores, you discover a significant need for intervention in a grade level. You have no budget to add programs, but these students need help.	1	2	3	4	5

Behavioral Challenges					
Concentration	Dread	Discomfort	Indifference	Engaged	Energized
You are called to address a belligerent student who is refusing to leave a classroom.	1	2	3	4	5
Students stage a walk out to protest a new school board policy.	1	2	3	4	5

The School Leader's Game Plan © 2025 Solution Tree Press • SolutionTree.com
Visit **go.SolutionTree.com/leadership** to download this free reproducible.

A fight breaks out between students in the cafeteria. You are short-staffed with administrators that day.	1	2	3	4	5
You receive word that a significant number of students are failing due to high absenteeism. You must respond within the next twenty-four hours.	1	2	3	4	5

Human Resources Challenges

Concentration	Dread	Discomfort	Indifference	Engaged	Energized
A staff member does not report to school on time, leaving their responsibilities uncovered.	1	2	3	4	5
A support staff member has been taken into police custody during non-work hours.	1	2	3	4	5
A staff member resigns three weeks into the school year. They give you no notice of their departure.	1	2	3	4	5
Due to a conflict in scheduling a professional development event, you discover that you do not have adequate staff to supervise students during lunch. The bell rings in fifteen minutes.	1	2	3	4	5

School Management Challenges

Concentration	Dread	Discomfort	Indifference	Engaged	Energized
Three days before the school year begins, you receive word that an influx of students will require you to reconfigure your schedule significantly.	1	2	3	4	5
An outbreak of sickness among support staff leaves your building short of appropriate classroom support for high-needs students. You must compose a short-term plan to respond.	1	2	3	4	5
As the school year starts, your teachers report that they are short on mandatory textbooks. You have no money left in your textbook account.	1	2	3	4	5
An extreme driver shortage renders your transportation provider unable to staff the bus routes. They don't know how long it will take to complete all routes.	1	2	3	4	5

Safety and Security Challenges

Concentration	Dread	Discomfort	Indifference	Engaged	Energized
You are responding to a report of an unidentified adult who has gained access to the building.	1	2	3	4	5
A fire alarm sounds just as students are entering the building in the morning. It's raining profusely.	1	2	3	4	5
During a routine evacuation drill, your staff discovers that there are three students missing from their classes. The fire department has not removed them as part of the drill.	1	2	3	4	5
Just as the bell rings for students to exit your building for recess (or dismissal), you receive a frantic call from duty staff that a bear has been sighted on school grounds.	1	2	3	4	5

Legal and Policy Challenges

Concentration	Dread	Discomfort	Indifference	Engaged	Energized
You receive a phone call from an attorney requesting a meeting with them and their clients, a family in your school, to discuss a matter regarding a cocurricular activity.	1	2	3	4	5
You are advised by your school board chair that you will be implementing a new student dress code when the school year starts in two weeks.	1	2	3	4	5
You have received word from your governing body that you have just three weeks to implement a new mandatory grading system in your school.	1	2	3	4	5
A community group reaches out to you to file a formal objection to the content of a book that is taught in your school.	1	2	3	4	5

Public Relations Challenges

Concentration	Dread	Discomfort	Indifference	Engaged	Energized
As you are preparing to dismiss students for the day, you are informed that a group of adults are forming a protest line outside of your main entrance. You do not know the subject of their protest.	1	2	3	4	5

The School Leader's Game Plan © 2025 Solution Tree Press • SolutionTree.com
Visit **go.SolutionTree.com/leadership** to download this free reproducible.

	Concentration	Dread	Discomfort	Indifference	Engaged	Energized
A local TV station reporter arrives in your office with a camera crew and asks if they can interview you about a disciplinary matter that has been reported to them by a community member.		1	2	3	4	5
You have twenty minutes to compose an email to parents regarding a controversial incident in your school.		1	2	3	4	5
You have been asked to deliver a speech at a national conference to a group of 5,000 of your fellow school leaders.		1	2	3	4	5

Major Weather or Environmental Incidents

	Concentration	Dread	Discomfort	Indifference	Engaged	Energized
A significant storm front is moving in while school is still in session. You must facilitate an early dismissal.		1	2	3	4	5
A weather emergency has resulted in power outages and school cancellation for what is expected to be at least two weeks. You have four hours to compose a response plan.		1	2	3	4	5
Your school experiences a water system malfunction—you have no water. You have ninety minutes to get it fixed or facilitate a dismissal.		1	2	3	4	5
While investigating a series of student and staff illnesses, you discover the presence of mold between the walls in a wing of your building.		1	2	3	4	5

Which categories cause you to engage to a greater degree?

Which ones do you dread or cause you to feel uncomfortable?

By identifying those areas that cause a negative reaction for you, you will be able to focus your attention on different means of reducing or focusing your reactions. Such techniques, which are discussed later in this book, include simulation and de-escalation. By developing a more detailed understanding of how you personally encounter stress, you will be able to personalize the work you do to prepare for it.

Explore ideas for preparing for stress reactions here.

A Path to Mindfulness, Authentic Reflection, and Self-Awareness

The following activity is intended to guide you in examining how you personally encounter stress and how your sympathetic reaction manifests itself in your daily life. It can be done silently by yourself or in a larger group with a facilitator reading the directions aloud. The idea is to try to maintain awareness of the exercise with as little wandering of your thoughts as possible. Your mind will wander—it's only natural that it does. By developing your ability to actively monitor the state of your body, you gain more accurate information regarding how you react to different situations and acquire valuable information that you can use to adapt to different stressors.

Begin by sitting comfortably and allowing your eyes to relax and focus on a single stationary point. If you're engaging in this activity alone, you can focus on the words on this page. Slow your body to relax as you focus on the instructions that follow.

1. Focus your attention on your right eye, then on your left.
2. Shift your focus to the top of your head. Is your head cold or warm?
3. Gradually shift your attention to the back of your neck. Feel any remaining tension leave the muscles that connect to your shoulders.
4. Move your attention down into your chest. Can you sense your heartbeat?
5. Shift your attention to your breathing. Try not to alter your breath pattern; just listen to the sound of the air entering and leaving your lungs.
6. As you breathe, does your chest expand or your abdomen?
7. Move your attention down to your abdomen. What are you feeling in your stomach right now? Can you hear any noises from your abdominal cavity?
8. Shift your attention to the points of contact between your body and the chair you are sitting on. Do you feel comfortable?
9. Bring your attention to your nostrils. Can you feel the air rushing in and out of your nose?
10. Return your focus to your eyes. Focus on your right eye, then on your left. Take a deep breath and bring your attention back to normal.

The point of this exercise is to check your ability to monitor your body systems through a mindful approach to attention. In an attempt to quiet thoughts about the past or future, focus on the present status of different systems within you, monitoring their state and function. While this activity can have a calming effect, it can also identify areas that may require closer attention. For example, if you are aware that your heart continues to race for a prolonged period following a stressful event, you may need a closer look from a physician or more cardiovascular exercise. Ultimately, this level of awareness can be beneficial in guiding you toward high-leverage variables in your effort to expand your leadership capacity.

As you begin to recognize both how you respond to stress and what works (or doesn't), you will begin to structure intentional support for this response. Your body is designed to respond to perceived threats, though the resulting allostatic load that comes from frequent or sustained stress will wear away at you over time. Armed with the awareness of how stress impacts you personally, answer the following questions.

- What techniques will work best for you to counteract the strain that a stress response places on your cardiovascular system?
- How can you structure your caloric input to counteract the release of glucose that comes with cortisol activation?
- What environmental cues would work best for you in the moments immediately following a stressful situation? Time alone versus time to talk to a trusted friend? Time outdoors versus a return to normal working conditions? Breathing techniques versus physical exercise? Are there other strategies that you value?

Capacity Overview Graphic Organizer

The following is intended to encourage you to review your current state of fitness and well-being in each of the following areas. This will assist you in differentiating where you are currently demonstrating competency and where you still need work. It establishes the broader view of variables impacting your work, which you will develop in detail in chapter 4 (page 73).

Please fill in each category with both your current practice and that to which you aspire.

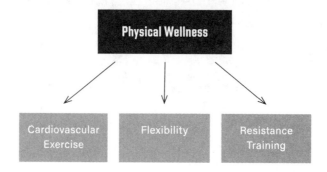

Current practice:

I wish I could:

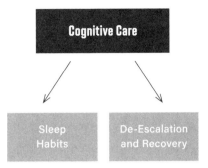

Current practice:

I wish I could:

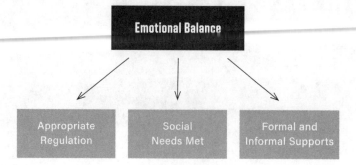

Current practice:

I wish I could:

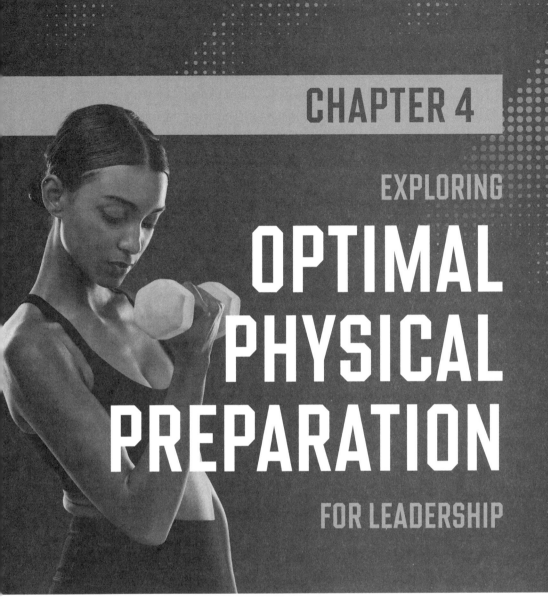

CHAPTER 4

EXPLORING OPTIMAL PHYSICAL PREPARATION FOR LEADERSHIP

Preparing for Stress

Athletes bring two aspects to their physical training: (1) their natural abilities and (2) the traits they develop over time. Both are important as an athlete rises through the levels of their respective competition. The higher they rise, the more specialized the training becomes. Focus shifts from fundamental skill development to more specialized training and tactics. Athletes develop a focus on metrics that indicate their ability to compete at higher levels, and they work to develop their performance in increasingly specific areas. They focus on components of their physical ability that will give them an advantage as differences between them and their competitors become more subtle.

While you are not necessarily competing against other leaders, you can learn something from the increasingly specialized approach to physical conditioning. Your body takes a beating, though of a vastly different sort. By learning more about what your work does to your body and by redefining the variables by which you measure your capacity within that environment, you can focus your attention on elements of your physical health that will directly impact your capacity to lead. You can train for the specific challenges, even if that training looks far different than it does currently. Where athletes focus their attention on the physical elements of their sport or event, leaders can focus on the impact of prolonged or frequent physiological responses to the stress of their work. Even though leadership jobs are not generally considered physically demanding, there's an impact of allostatic load over time. While seemingly manageable in the moment, you will see how your own ongoing physical reaction to stress can deplete your capacity if not managed properly. There are steps you can take to sustain yourself in this environment, but you need to recognize the value of doing so. Physical conditioning in athletics equates to the specialized program that leaders develop to remain effective in their roles.

Few people in leadership roles would deny the benefits of physical fitness. The problem, for many of us, is that there doesn't seem to be time in the day to accommodate it. Even if there was time, you may be reluctant to be seen exercising during the school day by some of your less supportive constituents, as you might appear to have too much time on your hands. For some, the lack of time to maintain a healthy degree of physical fitness is a badge of honor. The workaholic mindset is so prevalent in school leadership that this exaggerated degree of work focus becomes an indicator of competency rather than a detraction to well-being and capacity. Leaders perceive this complete focus on work time as either an expectation of the job or a sign of their level of commitment. Minimizing physical wellness to this degree indicates a more narrow focus on the appearance of leadership as opposed to the optimal functioning. Like many other elements of leaders' personal lives, they overlook things they consider to be of secondary importance when building schedules. Fitness becomes a luxury for which they have no time.

This continues until their level of physical well-being deteriorates to a point where poor health begins to impact their ability to effectively perform their responsibilities. Physical illness or chronic pain can impact a leader's ability to attend to their daily responsibilities. Leaders simply can't be completely present when they are sick or in pain. At best, they are distracted from their responsibilities. At worst, they become incapable of maintaining a fully functional role at all.

Of all the variables that impact a leader's performance, physical well-being is the most impactful and most frequently ignored. On a purely intuitive level, factors such as pain, nutrition, physical energy, or fatigue all affect work each day to varying degrees. The result is a pattern of distractibility or diminished motivation that often is written off as just part of the job as leaders power through full and stressful days.

Focus and attention would look vastly different if leaders viewed physical fitness and well-being as key components of maintaining the capacity to perform their job responsibilities. Leaders can benefit from understanding the physiological impact of prolonged stress on the body, and by demonstrating their understanding of basic components for addressing these responses. Because removing stress from the leadership role is simply not practical, leaders need to prepare to work within it at the most optimal level possible. Physical well-being will become an expectation of leaders instead of a luxury. This chapter discusses preparing for increased stress response and how exercising, eating healthy foods, dealing with illness appropriately, and spending time outdoors can help leaders build capacity and resilience to stress.

The days of a school leader are more than full, and demands on your time are a part of the role. The reproducible, "Carving Out Time for Activity" (page 88), is intended to look at different opportunities or windows of time when you can prioritize physical activity to help maintain your leadership capacity. A key is to be open to different possibilities, no matter how small they might seem.

Preparing for Increased Stress Response

Building physiological resilience within the scope of a leadership role begins with a clear understanding of how stress changes your body. A description of that process was detailed in chapter 3 (page 49) by examining autonomic responses and the concept of allostatic load. While the biochemistry of this process is complicated, fundamental parts of the stress reaction speak to elements of your physical condition that are within your control.

Consider the main components of the sympathetic nervous system. Dopamine, norepinephrine, and (ultimately) cortisol cause you to react in preparation for a fight-or-flight response. Blood flow is diverted away from bodily functions such as energy storage, digestion, and reproduction in favor of our brain and skeletal muscles (Harvard Health Publishing, 2024). This brings immediately needed oxygen and glucose to these two systems, which are at the core of your stress response. With energy storage paused, the body cannot look to fat reserves for glucose, so it extracts what is available from the liver and muscle tissue, which are open for business. The immune system is paused, and there is a momentary spike in inflammation just in case something is injured in its absence (American Psychological Association, 2018; Sapolsky, 2004). The body is now primed to fight or flee. These adaptations are a big help when reacting to a real threat but less so when you perceive a threat that isn't dangerous or is one you perceive on an ongoing basis (figure 4.1).

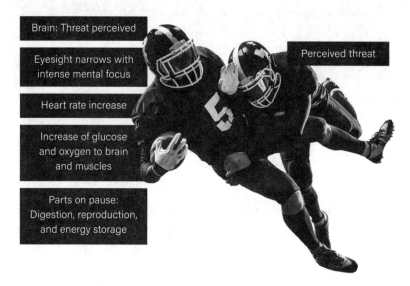

Source: *Adapted from Chu et al., 2024; Harvard Health Publishing, 2024; Sapolsky, 2004.*
FIGURE 4.1: What happens to the body when it's under stress.

So, what happens when there is neither fight nor flight? Your body is prepared for both options, so your pulse rate and blood pressure are elevated, your bloodstream is teeming with glucose, and a host of other physical reactions associated with this response are clicking. They are not burned off even if the stressor is psychologically induced or if the required reaction to the stressor is muted by a professional environment (Kramer et al., 2022). Your metaphorical engines are primed and revved, but you aren't going anywhere.

The impact of this reaction remains. Your body will de-escalate once the perceived threat has passed, and the parasympathetic response has an opportunity to activate. Glucose, floating freely in the bloodstream, will be stored once again, though not where it came from. The fat cells reopen for business, and that's where the glucose is headed. Muscle tissue remains tense, inflammation lingers throughout the body, and the cardiovascular system begins a slow process of recovery from the pressure placed on it (Harvard Health Publishing, 2024; Sapolsky, 2004). Overall, the resulting wear on your body is the price you pay for the response.

As a leader, many stressful events are beyond your control; how can you best manage the impact of this reaction? A solution begins with acknowledging those elements of your environment that are or are not in your control. Genetics, environment, and external parts of a situation are not in your control. Those are components you can navigate as best you can, strengthened by a focus on those factors you can influence. What you can control is preparing your body to withstand the impact of stressful situations while remaining as healthy as possible. To be healthy means strengthening the cardiovascular system, managing glucose levels, introducing healthy fuel into your body, and offsetting the impact of inflammation (Burn, 2020). In other words, focus on diet and exercise.

Getting Started With Exercise

For some leaders, exercise is an integral part of their day. They already recognize the positive impact that it has on nearly all elements of their well-being. For others, it is something that almost feels like an allergy or at least an unrealistic aspiration. Most are somewhere in the middle. This wide range of fitness speaks to the point made in chapter 2 (page 29), where the process of planning for physical health is personalized and competency based. So, if one person runs ultramarathons on the weekend, then competency has been demonstrated. On the other hand, another person might be winded by climbing a flight of stairs. For that person, physical fitness becomes an area of focus that is well worth their consideration for increasing their leadership capacity. Improved physical fitness will improve their ability to endure repeated or prolonged stress reactions while remaining healthy and working at optimal levels within their professional role. Therefore, cardiovascular exercise may be an appropriate element of a professional development plan.

In addition, there is a substantial connection between regular exercise and a healthier relationship with stress. From a metabolic standpoint, cardiovascular exercise assists the body in burning off the excess glucose released during the sympathetic stress response. It strengthens the heart and lowers the blood pressure, thereby helping you endure escalations and reduce damage during stressful situations. More efficient processing of oxygen in the lungs even helps to minimize the strain on the pulmonary system as well, thereby reducing the amount of allostatic load on the lungs and respiration (Holmes, 2022). In short, regular physical exercise increases the body's ability to handle stress and remain healthy. Naturally, there are cognitive and emotional benefits to exercise as well (chapters 5 and 6, pages 91 and 103).

When starting from scratch with a program for cardiovascular fitness, it is always advisable to visit a doctor. Regular wellness visits include a baseline measurement of fitness through metrics like blood pressure, pulse rate, and a panel of blood tests, which can give your physician an indication of what cardiovascular exercises would be the best starting points. Including a physician in this process is crucial because you are basing a component of your growth as a leader on this effort. While fitness watches and apps are good interim monitors of progress, reliable data are essential, and physician-provided data are the most reliable. Further, there is at least the possibility of a preexisting or chronic condition. No one really knows, in detail, the current condition of their heart or circulatory system independently of a physician's insights. By identifying and thoroughly understanding any underlying challenges you may have been facing without your awareness, you free up the mental space to engage in the process with a higher degree of commitment and enthusiasm. It all starts with an accurate picture of your foundation.

One of the more promising metrics for personal well-being and sympathetic-parasympathetic balance is *heart rate variability* (HRV). HRV quantifies the variations in the spaces between your heartbeats (Haskell et al., 2007). Though you may think that a consistent heartbeat is a good thing, you have very small variations between each beat that indicate the health of your autonomic nervous system. More specifically, a higher HRV reveals the efficiency with which your body can adapt between a sympathetic and a parasympathetic response (you'll remember these as your stress and de-stress responses, respectively). In other words, a higher HRV score indicates that the body can move in and out of stress more efficiently.

Whether or not you're familiar with the concept of HRV, chances are you have a means of measuring it right on your wrist. Most smartwatches or fitness trackers now include a feature that measures HRV within their heart-monitoring capabilities, giving you access to this helpful piece of insight regarding your heart health and stress adaptation.

According to the American Heart Association, you should aim for 150–180 minutes of moderate cardiovascular exercise per week (U.S. Department of Health and Human Services, 2018). This is a level of exercise that forces you to breathe hard but not so much that you can't speak. Think of a social run, bike ride, or game of tennis. You should be breathing hard, but you should also be able to chat with your friends as you exercise. The result is a moderate but appropriate amount of strain placed on your heart and blood vessels, resulting in both becoming stronger and more resilient over time.

Once you are fitted with an appropriate exercise program, you can begin to use the metrics inherent in that activity to chart your progress. Exercise machines such as treadmills or stair steppers make measurement and incremental improvement even easier. Yoga practice is easily modified to suit your ability level as you progress. More advanced activities provide equally useful manners of tracking progress—longer distances or quicker times for runners or swimmers, heavier weights for lifters, or greater challenges for participants in CrossFit workouts all become a means of quantifying progress. Ultimately, the point is to find a cardiovascular exercise that you enjoy and can sustain and a means of measuring progress.

A key element to sustaining any exercise is to find something that you enjoy doing. Humans are averse to drudgery, so choosing an activity you dread simply for effect will not be sustainable. By beginning with the goal in mind—to elevate your heart rate to invoke cardiovascular exercise—you move into an examination of potential forms of exercise that are both interesting to you and sustainable given the time and constraints of your day. Of course, you should select an activity that is commensurate with your fitness level and consistent with your doctor's approval. The key is to start small and choose an activity that is appropriate for you. By starting with an achievable goal in an activity you enjoy, you'll increase your likelihood of sticking to it. If you schedule something you look forward to, you greatly improve the potential of sustaining the benefits.

According to exercise experts Iñigo San Millán and Peter Attia, in their conversation on Attia's (2022) podcast, a difference can be made in your personal fitness at three to four days per week at thirty minutes per session of zone 2 cardio. This designation of exercise refers to a person exerting themselves at 60–70 percent of their maximum heart rate. For comparison, this level of exertion results in increased pulse and breathing, but still allows you to carry on a conversation (Attia, 2022). This hardly bears resemblance to an intense workout, yet you are strengthening your cardiovascular system.

Even when you have the best intentions to exercise, there may be times when you simply may not be able to commit to a regular workout program. Does this mean you are off the hook for some form of movement? Not if you want to increase your physical resilience. It is possible to build movement into your day in other forms. Walking more, taking the stairs, or other forms of intentional movement breaks are all ways to make some progress. In this respect, fitness trackers become a solid source for data and inspiration. These devices provide the measurements discussed earlier (even if not wholly reliable) while recognizing the importance of well-being. Many health insurance plans provided by school districts also include wellness programs, even providing funds to purchase these fitness trackers at reduced rates. The following are a few ways to increase the number of minutes during which you experience increased cardiovascular load within the school day.

- Schedule a hall-duty period when you walk through the school at pace, including stairs where possible, which increases both active minutes and visibility within the school.

- Circulate among after-school activities, including both indoor and outdoor activities, engaging with students and staff while moving at pace.

- Schedule moving meetings with members of your team where discussions and information can be shared without the need to sit for long periods of time.

- Transition between classes or meetings where no increment of time is too small. Passing times, recesses, or lunch periods are all opportunities to move in a manner that elevates our heart rate.

- Join in with classes that are engaged in movement-based activities, whether physical education, outdoor activities, or transitions. Even five to ten minutes makes a difference.

By incorporating elements of movement into your day, you can increase your own physical resilience while providing a positive example to staff and students alike about the importance of prioritizing wellness. Ideally, you also create space beyond the school day to engage in some other form of exercise that gives you greater headspace and allows for positive reframing. In the end, you are looking to add time to each day to exercise your cardiovascular system in appropriate and sustainable ways. It is a practice linked directly to your efforts to sustain your capacity to lead.

The reproducible, "An Inventory of How You Are Feeling" (page 89), is intended to encourage you to take a step back and consider your overall health in a holistic sense. By focusing on a more general or comprehensive view of how your body works, you can focus on new elements to increase your capacity to work at your best.

Choosing Healthy Foods

Most practicing educators are a source of entertainment for our non-educator friends at dinner parties because our friends do not work in an environment in which they have eighteen minutes to eat. For educators and school staff, food is functional, and the window of available time is small. Nutrition is nice, but it is often a luxury. However, food can be among the most useful tools for maintaining optimal levels of functioning at work. What you eat, as well as what you don't eat, are equally relevant when it comes to building a resilient body. Of all the different components of leadership capacity, diet may be the one with the greatest need for personalization. It can take more money, time, and commitment to make better food choices, but the benefits can make it worthwhile. The following are some widely held, fundamental principles to be aware of when choosing foods.

- **The less processed the food, the healthier it is:** Eating foods that have been through minimal processing is a great start. When possible, choosing organic or sustainable meats and dairy products, an array of vegetables and low-sugar fruits, and whole or sprouted grains is an excellent choice for better health. When reading ingredients lists, look for products containing whole foods, especially those listed as the first ingredients. Ever wonder why food that would normally be refrigerated can sit on a shelf without spoiling? Chances are that something has been added to the food to make that possible. You are well served to know what that additive is and what impact it could have on your body (Albuquerque, Bragotto, & Costa, 2022; Fuhrman, 2018). For most people, healthier food choices can be found by shopping the perimeter of a grocery store, which is where unprocessed foods are traditionally found.

- **Sugar has very little nutritional benefit:** While the body does require some glucose to function, there is plenty of it in a standard diet. Knowing how your body uses sugar is a solid starting point to understanding your wider metabolism. Also remember that cortisol causes the body to set free a flood of glucose into the bloodstream that often goes unused and stored again in less healthy places. Then, there is the accompanying insulin spike. All of these factors impact the way your body functions (Freeman et al., 2018; Shanahan & Shanahan, 2017).

What makes sugar problematic is a process called glycation. Sugar coats your cell membranes as it seeps into your tissues, causing health issues, including impairing mood and memory; stiffening of collagen in your tendons, bones, and skin; damaging your white blood cells; and interfering with hormone receptors. Carbohydrates are also a form of sugar and convert to simple sugars during digestion. Refined carbs are plentiful in a Western diet, and they have been stripped of all bran, fiber, and nutrients that slow down absorption. Therefore, they digest quickly and lead to unhealthy spikes in blood sugar levels. The least complicated way to reduce or eliminate sugar and refined carbs in your diet is to check food labels on everything you buy to monitor sugar content (Freeman et al., 2018; Shanahan & Shanahan, 2017).

- **Know what's in your food:** If you can't pronounce the name of an ingredient, you probably should know a little more about where it came from. A quick glance at a food label will tell you how much of it was produced on a farm versus in a lab. The addition of hard-to-pronounce food dyes, preservatives, thickeners, emulsifiers, sugar substitutes, and natural flavors in food is widespread in the United States. Nearly all of these additives turn healthy, whole foods into inflammation-promoting empty calories (Center for Science in the Public Interest, n.d.). You can limit the long-term effects of these ingredients by staying aware of them and choosing less-processed foods (Center for Science in the Public Interest, n.d.). While regulatory agencies do approve these ingredients for consumption, that doesn't mean that those ingredients will support your desire for a healthier diet. It is helpful to know what those ingredients are doing to you (U.S. Food and Drug Administration, 2023).

- **Choose healthy oils:** Like sugar, oils get their own spot on this list because of their widespread use in food and the wide range of health impacts they have. In this case, the distinction lies both in the type of oil and the way it has been processed. Some oils are derived from pressing the fruit (avocado or olive oils) while others must be chemically extracted (most seed oils). By understanding these processes, you will be able to discern the health impacts for your specific dietary choices (Shanahan, 2020). Most commonly, the "good" ones include olive oil, coconut oil, avocado oil, and butter. Industrial seed oils, such as canola, cottonseed, corn, soy, safflower, and sunflower oil, are chemically treated and should be avoided (Shanahan, 2020).

- **Be aware of the connection between food and inflammation:** The immune system generates inflammation in response to perceived threats or damage. What happens when this reaction is generated by something you eat? Your body can react similarly to food as it would to any other injury. Certain foods, such as ultra-processed foods or red meat, are well-established causes of inflammation even in the absence of a stress response (McDonald, 2020). Their effect makes stress-related inflammation even more severe and difficult to get rid of. By being aware of the different foods impacting inflammation, you can take steps to avoid these where possible to minimize their impact in the short term. According to nutrition expert Edwin McDonald (2020)—

  > People really need to focus on their pattern of eating—as opposed to eating a few particular foods—to reduce inflammation. There's no miracle food out there that's going to cure people with chronic inflammation. You need to have an anti-inflammatory lifestyle and diet.

While the prior list is not exhaustive, it highlights some of the key elements of food intake that affect your overall levels of functioning and health. Food can fuel you in positive ways, but it can also be a detriment when you introduce unhealthy substances into your body.

While an integral part of the preceding list, inflammation is worthy of further consideration as you identify potential areas to increase your capacity. Dietary inflammation only adds to the stress on the body that comes with allostatic load and frequent or prolonged stress reactions (see chapter 3, page 49). One of the outcomes mentioned earlier in this book is how the immune system reacts to stress. As a reminder, the sympathetic response takes energy that would be committed to healing and recovery and reallocates it to the fight-or-flight response. The immune system temporarily suspends operations. Before shutting down, the immune system releases leukocytes to incite a measure of inflammation, just in case injury is possible due to this threat (Chu et al., 2024). That inflammation will remain until the full measure of the parasympathetic response has had the opportunity to take hold (Sapolsky, 2004). Inflammation is the body's mechanism for responding to injury and initiating healing. Sounds like a good system, right?

Acute inflammation is a typical response to an injury within the body. It starts, it heals, and it goes away. However, ongoing and frequent stress inflammation may not subside. The body crosses over from a more functional acute inflammation response into a chronic or ongoing response. In addition to stress, that condition can be made worse by ingesting foods that promote inflammation on a broader scale throughout the body (Cleveland Clinic, n.d.). In this case, inflammation does not go away with the end of the stressor, and the body's immune response begins to impact healthy cells within the body.

Inflammation is a significant factor in many diseases that afflict human beings, yet that impact goes largely unacknowledged. Medical conditions such as type 2 diabetes, rheumatoid arthritis, and even dementia all count among the causes of inflammation within the body (Rohleder, 2019). If you attempt to build a healthier approach to maintaining your leadership capacity, understanding the impact inflammation has on your personal well-being becomes a foundational element of your plan. Cardiovascular exercise and the resulting increase in circulatory health allow the body to de-escalate an inflammatory response more efficiently, and you can minimize or eliminate foods from your diet that cause inflammation.

Naturally, any discussion of food and diet will land somewhere on the topic of weight loss. Speaking in terms of general health, weight loss is a well-established means of supporting overall health and well-being and can certainly be included within the context of leadership capacity. Due to the highly individualized nature of body weight and composition, I've chosen not to delve into the details within this book; there are countless volumes about weight loss, diet, and eating styles. I do acknowledge that a substantive weight-loss program, under appropriate medical supervision, can certainly be an element of maintaining your capacity to lead. This is a topic best discussed with your health care provider with consideration of your overall health history and individual goals.

Taking a more active approach to understanding the impact certain foods or ingredients have on your metabolism allows you to see food as fuel that powers your desire to work at optimal levels.

Dealing With Sickness

Physical illness impacts leadership performance in terms of work attendance and how leaders work while sick to maintain performance even when they are at a lesser capacity. Most leaders will try to push through times when they are not feeling their best. That work ethic is often what allows them to rise to leadership positions. Leaders keep showing up. They persevere. They work when they aren't feeling well, and sometimes that is necessary. Other times, though, it is a detriment. Therefore, leaders must ask if they can see the difference.

There are two fundamental sources of information to guide you when you are working at a diminished capacity and might need time to step away. You can rely on your own self-awareness and interoception (an awareness of internal sensations in the body), or you can rely on your colleagues. Like competitive athletes, leaders don't want to step out of the game if they can continue at some diminished level of performance, yet doing so might be in the best interest of the team. They push through out of commitment, even overriding their interoception and self-awareness. Therefore, this leaves leaders to rely on the second source of information—their team. By maintaining a degree of professional comfort and trust, you can listen when others say it is time to step away. There is always a time to put up your hand and call for a substitution. By acknowledging your diminished capacity, you respond to your commitment to the organization you lead; it is your responsibility as a leader to step aside and restore yourself to full health before reentering the game.

Some chronic health conditions are reversible or manageable. Most commonly, conditions such as hypertension, obesity, arthritis, type 2 diabetes, addiction, and depression are known to be linked to prolonged or chronic exposure to stress (Yale Medicine, n.d.). Each of these conditions can present life-altering challenges that begin with an impact on leaders' work and extend into the larger issue of quality of life. Addressing these health issues begins under the guidance of an appropriate health care professional and is beyond the scope of a conventional program of diet and exercise.

Chronic health conditions can present a challenge to school leaders that requires a specific program of care. However, they by no means signal the end of a leader's effectiveness. Just as with any other variable that impacts physical capacity, the road forward begins with acknowledging the issue, taking active steps to address it, or putting mechanisms in place to enable coping with or accommodating it. Here again, postponing treatment for or recovery from chronic health challenges to attend to your leadership responsibilities limits your overall capacity. Chronic health conditions should not be ignored or hidden. Acknowledging their impact and working actively with your health care provider on approved treatments can represent an opportunity for you to expand your capacity and enrich your life.

Spending Time Outdoors

The great outdoors means different things to different people. For some, the outdoors is an escape—something you long for as you stare out the window from a meeting. For others, time outdoors is a world filled with insects and wild animals, devoid of climate control. In the world of educational leadership, these viewpoints are amplified by the students. Anyone unsure what this means has never experienced a rainy-day indoor recess in an elementary school. Our younger learners need to roam—maybe we do too.

Does spending time outside actually improve your ability to de-escalate and restore normal functioning? Yes! In a 2014 literature review, the conclusion indicates a consistent degree of stress de-escalation in outdoor, predominantly natural environments as opposed to similar circumstances in urban settings (Berto, 2014). Another review of research cites a strengthened immune system, endorphin release, and improved mood among the health benefits of time spent outdoors (Intermountain Health, 2020). The National Institutes of Health makes a similar assertion in a study published in their National Library of Medicine, titled "The Health Benefits of the Great Outdoors: A Systematic Review and Meta-Analysis of Greenspace Exposure and Health Outcomes." According to this meta-analysis, the study concludes that, "Greenspace exposure is associated with numerous health benefits in intervention and observational studies" (Twohig-Bennett & Jones, 2018). Time spent outdoors, in whatever form, has a positive impact on health (even despite insects and wild animals).

Although the ability to spend time outdoors may be limited by many factors, including where you live and your access to natural environments, the fact remains that it can be a viable means of de-escalating stress reactions and maintaining optimal levels of physical health. A 2020 study from an interdisciplinary team from Cornell University shows that college students were able to benefit from outdoor time in as little as ten minutes (Cordova, 2020). They also extended their study to outdoor time at urban universities (Cordova, 2020). Allowing yourself time to be exposed to whatever nature is available outside of your respective building also means you create space from your office and the responsibilities within. Even if your school is in a more urban setting, prioritizing outdoor time also prioritizes your well-being. It is a time-out from the pace of your day. The next chapter will help you with getting quality sleep and dealing with fatigue.

Questions for Reflection

Use the following questions to help you reflect on what you have read in this chapter.

1. How much of a priority is physical fitness for you? What opportunities fit into you schedule? How might you expand your time windows to prioritize fitness?

2. What activities do you enjoy but don't have time to participate in them? How might you reintroduce them into your life as a component of maintaining your leadership capacity?

3. Are you aware of any groups, classes, or communities that participate in a wellness activity that you'd like to join? If so, how might you reprioritize time to participate. If not, where might you locate information on such groups?

4. How carefully do you monitor the food you eat and what impact it may have on your sense of well-being and professional capacity? What would you like to learn more about related to food and diet?

5. How much time do you spend outside each day? What outdoor activities are available to you in your home or work environments? What approaches might you take to free up more time for outdoor activities?

Carving Out Time for Activity

Time is valuable to school leaders; it's an absolute given. You simply never have enough of it to answer all the demands you face. With that acknowledged, the overall benefits of cardiovascular exercise are so important for maintaining capacity that carving out even a modicum of time to move is a step in the right direction.

Please use the following chart to examine your daily schedule and find opportunities for movement that result in zone 2 cardiovascular activity as defined in this chapter—elevated heart rate while you're still able to hold a conversation.

- Walk, jog, or cycle
- Morning exercise class or home workout

- Moving meetings, duties, or visibility
- Active breaks or group activities
- School activities involving movement

- Staff groups or fitness activities
- Independent exercise

Where can you fit in more opportunities to emphasize physical activities?

_____
_____
_____
_____

What current activities can you either combine or reschedule to make time for this?

_____
_____
_____
_____

This process begins with prioritizing movement over the course of your day. You can become an example of prioritizing fitness and practice a healthier lifestyle in the process.

An Inventory of How You Are Feeling

The process of reflecting on your physical well-being begins with understanding your current state of health. The following resources can guide you in that process and provide a sense of direction as you look to optimize your physical health.

1. **Schedule a consultation and comprehensive physical exam with a health care provider:** This includes a substantive acknowledgment of the stressful nature of your work, and a consultation regarding the ways your work has affected your physical health.
    - When was your last physical exam with your doctor?
    - What advice were you given? Have you followed that advice?
    - What barriers are there in your day that prevent you from practicing self-care and fitness at this level?

2. **Evaluate and reflect on any chronic or limiting health conditions you may be struggling with:** Often, the inflammation resulting from frequent stress activation can worsen the impact of chronic health problems. If left unaddressed, these health complications can wear away at your capacity over the long term, diminishing your effectiveness.
    - Do you have any existing health conditions that impact your physical or cognitive capacity within your work?
    - What can be done, within your control, to lessen or better cope with these conditions?
    - What additional supports or strategies might reduce this impact?

3. **Establish measurable goals relative to your current and aspirational level of health and fitness:** This includes cardiovascular fitness, weight, body composition, muscular strength, and flexibility.
    - What activities do you enjoy that might also be considered cardiovascular exercise (elevated heart rate and breathing hard)?
    - Are there activities you have always wanted to try, but you've never been able to? How might you make time for these experiences?
    - How might you increase your level of physical conditioning in even the smallest, least-invasive ways? Small changes lead to big differences!

page 1 of 2

The School Leader's Game Plan © 2025 Solution Tree Press • SolutionTree.com
Visit **go.SolutionTree.com/leadership** to download this free reproducible.

4. **Your schedule reveals your priorities:** Review your daily, weekly, or recurring schedule to identify when you have some available time. Given the importance of prioritizing physical fitness as a component of leadership capacity, when can you schedule regular opportunities for physical activity? There is no such thing as starting too small.

    - When might you be able to build in time to exercise for ten minutes?
    - What activities already exist during your day that might allow you to move more?
    - Who might you be able to partner with to introduce more movement and physical activity into your daily schedule?
    - What types of physical activities or exercises do you truly enjoy but currently are unable to practice? Look for ways to schedule even occasional or variable alternatives to this activity.

5. **What can you learn about physical well-being or fitness that will help you expand your physical capacity?** Identify potential areas for extended study or learning that impact this area and build them into your plan for professional development.

    - Is there a new sport or activity you'd like to learn about?
    - Is there an activity that you used to enjoy that you no longer practice?
    - What areas of exercise or physical capacity interest you? By learning more about how your body works, you find additional chances or activities that might lead to fitness opportunities.

CHAPTER 5
GETTING QUALITY SLEEP
AND DEALING WITH FATIGUE

Managing Energy as a Finite Resource

Competitive athletes rise to those levels because they have a distinct understanding of their gifts and how best to put them to use within their chosen sport. For a leader, the single most important tool you have is your brain. You are called on to use it in a dizzying variety of ways throughout your day, and if, for some reason, it is not working well, you will know it quickly. So, what can you learn from elite athletes about how best to condition your mind? The key lies in understanding energy as a finite resource.

As their understanding of training and competition grows, athletes come to view energy as a resource. In this case, energy refers both to physical energy and cognitive and emotional resilience. Expend too much energy in training and the athlete will overtrain and be depleted when it's time to compete. Expend too little and their training will be insufficient, leaving them inadequately prepared. The key to achieving optimal levels of performance is to find the balance point somewhere in the middle—the athlete is as prepared as possible and yet properly energized for the demands of competition. As a perfect illustration, many marathon runners cite the mental wear of a 26.2-mile race as one of their greatest challenges. Where the race can involve three or four hours (or more) of mental tedium blended with extreme physical exertion, deploying energy becomes central to their success. They are challenged to parse out physical energy in a measured, gradual way while maximizing mental engagement to remain focused. They must have enough physical energy to finish the race while maintaining mental focus and awareness of their position in the course. If they lose focus mentally, they will not be able to succeed physically, and vice versa. Leaders can learn something from this example, even if they have no intention of ever running a marathon.

Your schedules and expectations can absolutely wear you out to a degree where you are depleted of energy, particularly cognitively. By taking the time to examine the elements of cognitive functioning and well-being, you can learn to prioritize your expenditure of mental energy and focus to sustain yourself over the course of a long and challenging school year. This won't happen by chance, though. A simple practice of adhering to all the demands you face will result in a long-term depletion of energy. Mirroring the practice of elite athletes and managing your cognitive energy over time will allow you to function at the outer limits of your potential.

Just as with the body, your stress reaction brings specific conditions to the way your brain functions, which is important to understand to build leadership capacity. Three neurochemicals guide the stressed brain. First, dopamine is known as a reward hormone; however, in this situation, it also increases our ability to focus on specific details. Second, norepinephrine (also known as noradrenaline in Europe) brings additional energy and alertness. Third, acetylcholine brings about a level of sharp focus (Fabritius & Hagemann, 2017).

In their book *The Leading Brain: Powerful Science-Based Strategies for Achieving Peak Performance*, Friederike Fabritius and Hans W. Hagemann (2017) describe this neurological process in this way:

> Think of it as a prizewinning photograph. Noradrenaline prompts you to point your camera in just the right direction, dopamine helps you to zoom in until you have a pleasing composition, and finally there's acetylcholine, which enables you to sharpen your focus until it's picture perfect. (p. 29)

In function, this means that you are energized, alert, and hyperfocused. Your peripheral vision dulls as you focus more intently on what's in front of you. The brain has passed control from the analytical prefrontal cortex to the more reactive amygdala. There's no need to spend too much time analyzing when there's a bear in front of you. Thanks to the physiological effects of cortisol and other chemicals, your bloodstream is flushed with oxygen and glucose, diverted to the brain from other systems that are less useful in a crisis (Fabritius & Hagemann, 2017). Your mind is highly reactive, energized, and focused, which is a very useful state amid an emergency. But, what about when you are trying to get a good night's rest? Certainly, these conditions are less helpful.

This leads the discussion to the elements of restoring cognitive and mental functioning for optimal leadership performance. Here, you have less direct control over the physiological conditioning of your brain compared to your cardiovascular system, and yet you are not powerless. You gain more leverage in maintaining a healthy brain by de-escalating and recovering from the long-term impact of stress reactions.

There are two key elements that have the greatest impact.

1. **Sleep quality:** The science on the importance of cognitive recovery is rock solid (Walker, 2017). Your brain will not function properly if you don't receive adequate amounts of quality sleep each day. In fact, your entire metabolism will not work well. Sleep is the daily opportunity for your brain to process the avalanche of data that your senses absorb each day, and the window of time during which the brain resets itself for the next day. Deprived of this opportunity, the brain will not function properly, and the body will follow (Walker, 2017).

2. **Cognitive de-escalation:** As previously mentioned, your autonomic nervous system is intricately designed to prepare your body for stressful situations that bring about a comprehensive metabolic shift. It also has mechanisms to return the body to a more normal or energy-efficient manner of operation. This reaction was designed for short and infrequent episodes of adaptation, not for ongoing or long-term operation. When your body (and in this case, specifically your brain) is subjected to stress repeatedly or over the long term, what was once

an advantage can quickly turn into a detriment in the face of allostatic load as discussed in chapter 3 (page 49). A healthy brain that functions at optimal levels has appropriate opportunities to de-escalate, refocus, and heal (Burn, 2020)

There are most certainly other variables that can fall under the category of optimal brain function, such as diet and exercise. This chapter explores sleep and the brain, bringing the brain back to balance using de-escalation strategies, and dealing with fatigue.

Exploring Sleep and the Brain

Ample research on sleep suggests that the brain is as active (and in some cases more so) in certain stages of sleep as it is when you are awake (Walker, 2017). According to sleep expert Matthew Walker (2017), sleep is a central element of health, cognitive functioning, longevity, and overall well-being. For the purposes of examining optimal conditions for leadership functioning, look at sleep from the perspective of how the brain works.

Sleep is a period of unconsciousness that occupies about one-third of every day. Sleep-wake cycles, known as *circadian rhythms*, are a normal part of the body's daily operation. You can only stay awake for so long before you succumb to the elevated levels of adenosine in your bloodstream, and you drift off into the recuperative state known as sleep (Walker, 2017).

Once asleep, the brain passes through different stages. What has emerged from sleep science is a more substantive understanding of the recuperative impact sleep has on the brain. As you pass through lighter sleep into deep sleep, your brain is busy sorting memories and sensory data compiled over the course of the past day. The brain resets itself both biochemically and by storing information. If allowed to do so in a complete manner, you awaken the next morning feeling sharp and ready to dive into another day (Walker, 2017).

The differentiation between sleep duration and sleep quality is among speculation. Do you need as much sleep if your sleep is restful? Is total time asleep more important than deep sleep? Which should you prioritize? The answer appears to be both. Your brain requires both time and depth of sleep to complete the cleaning process. You can't shorten one without harming the overall picture (Walker, 2017).

Walker (2017) asserts that nearly everyone requires seven to nine hours of sleep each night to support healthy physical and cognitive functioning. You can expect to see significant impacts on your health if you receive fewer than six hours per night. According to Walker (2017), "Routinely sleeping less than six hours a night weakens your immune system, substantially increases your risk of certain forms of cancer" (p. 3). He then elaborates on the links between shortened sleep and Alzheimer's disease, diabetes, and heart disease. In short, lack of sleep is no joke. It has been substantially connected to a dizzying number of health factors. In this way, sleep is more than just a crucial component to cognitive functioning. It is a foundational element of overall health.

One common misconception about sleep is the idea that you can simply make up for lost or imperfect sleep by sleeping more the next night or by pushing through times of short sleep in hopes of improvement over time. Here, Walker's (2017) research is quite clear that, instead, you accumulate a sleep debt over lost sleep due primarily to the accumulation of adenosine in your body: "Like an outstanding debt on a loan, come morning, some quantity of yesterday's adenosine remains. You carry that outstanding sleep balance throughout the day. Also like a loan in arrears, this sleep debt will continue to accumulate" (p. 35). As such, the only way for you to recover from poor sleep is by establishing consistent, quality sleep patterns over time. You can't just power through and hope to recover quickly.

On the functional side, everyone has experienced the mental fallout from imperfect sleep. While it has been substantiated by research, you probably didn't need that backup to know that sleep deprivation brings with it distractibility, irritability, and short-term memory challenges (Suni & Vyas, 2023). All of these side effects have the potential to impact your work during a full school day. School leaders are expected to engage in fast decision making, complex communication, and reflective problem solving, which are more challenging in the fog of sleep deprivation.

On the positive side, one term that recurs frequently in sleep improvement circles is the concept of *sleep hygiene*, which is made up of the various conditions that increase the likelihood of a positive sleep session. These conditions include environmental factors, such as darkness and cooler temperatures, as well as refraining from caffeine or alcohol (Walker, 2017). As you try to optimize your sleep pattern, these practices and others associated with them help you to minimize behavioral or environmental factors that may be hurting your sleep. This concept is explored further in the reproducible "Sleep Hygiene Checklist" (page 102). The short-term and long-term benefits of sleep are so familiar, so why are leaders quick to accept a shortage of it as a part of their work?

Ask any school leader how they slept last night. You'll most likely receive a response punctuated by a chuckle, an eye roll, or outright disdain. Healthy sleep is considered to be among the early casualties of accepting a leadership position in schools. If you do encounter one of the fortunate few who do sleep well, you might regard them with envy at the very least or blatant contempt at most.

This is a direct reflection of the stress leaders encounter during their daily work. It's known that the brain can bring about a stress response in the face of threats that are either anticipated or remembered. It's the same when you are trying to drift off to sleep. The stress reaction is the same as with a bear under your bed. With an influx of energy, focused attention, and nutrients to the brain, it is little wonder that you often struggle to drift off to sleep for a full night.

In some circles, sleep deprivation is even worn like a badge of honor. It is offered in conversation as evidence of a leader's endurance under stress. "I only slept three hours last night!" is offered as a point of commiseration among leaders around morning coffee. Like many other stress-related health concerns, leaders minimize these concerns and shrug them off as fallout from their commitment to their work. Little attention is given to the impact of this coping mechanism, and the results linger on and impede leaders' capacities. They simply aren't as prepared for the work as they could be.

What, then, does a lack of sleep do to you in the long term? According to Walker (2017), "Every major system, tissue, and organ in your body suffers when sleep becomes short. No aspect of your health can retreat at the sign of sleep loss and escape unharmed" (p. 164). Sleep is a central factor in your overall health, notably in how your brain functions (Suni & Vyas, 2023). Each day, the brain produces adenosine as a by-product of energy processing. As it builds up in the brain, adenosine receptors track the amount present. The more adenosine in the brain, the sleepier you feel (Bryan & Adavadkar, 2023). The brain is telling you that it needs to shut down to tidy up a bit. This is also a good time to discuss caffeine. This popular morning elixir binds to adenosine receptors, blocking them from doing their normal work. This results in feeling more awake, but it doesn't remove the adenosine. That is why you often feel a crash once the caffeine wears off. That adenosine is still there, waiting patiently to bring on that rush of fatigue and sleep pressure. Whether you heed it or not is another matter (Bryan & Adavadkar, 2023; Walker, 2017).

Your ability to invoke appropriate judgment in your work is central to leadership. All leaders are expected to execute sound decision making, regardless of the nature of their position or circumstances. Attention span is an element of good judgment and a fundamental interpersonal skill for establishing positive working relationships with those around us. Simply put, leaders are expected to pay attention and make sound decisions, particularly in organizations that are fundamentally constructed around people like schools.

Many biological processes that impact sleep and wake states are connected to circadian rhythm. These patterns allow the different systems in our physical makeup to cycle in and out of functioning and recovery in sync with the hours in a day. The body has sensors that impact the direction of resources according to the time of day based on light sensitivity and internal energy use.

Circadian rhythm is the way our brain tells time. It uses sensory cues, such as daylight, food intake, and the accumulation of biochemical substances like adenosine and melatonin, to determine the most appropriate degree of wakefulness (Walker, 2017). From this pattern, the other systems of the brain and body can regulate their degree of function for things like hunger, body temperature, and fatigue (Bryan & Guo, 2024).

Leaders often find themselves working against this natural pattern of functioning as they attempt to find balance in the face of physical challenges resulting from stressful work. Early starts, long days, and working nights force the body into an unnatural rhythm in defiance of adenosine load and energy depletion (Walker, 2017). Leaders push through because they must. This only adds to the allostatic load on the body, with depletion compounding by the hour and day. To accommodate for this diminished state, people often force their bodies into an artificial rhythm by ingesting substances, such as food, drink, or drugs, that either postpone fatigue or boost energy artificially. Some drink coffee to wake up in the morning, eat unhealthy foods due to convenience or satiety, calm their nerves at the end of the day with a cocktail, and force themselves to sleep with some form of sleep aid (Walker, 2017). Leaders know that each element of this process is part of a balanced and healthy lifestyle, yet the way it's achieved is anything but healthy. There are promises to keep, and little time for adherence to that internal circadian clock.

A path forward begins with awareness. Keeping in mind the goal of increased cognitive capacity, it is possible to take small, manageable steps toward this healthy balance if done deliberately. After all, how you allocate time is a clear indication of what is most valuable to you. When it comes to sleep, small benefits add up quickly. Taking steps like sticking to a regular sleep schedule or optimizing your sleep environment allows your body to experience the rejuvenating elements of higher-quality sleep. Committing to a form of intentional de-escalation that is most effective for you, such as outdoor time, meditation, or physical activity, denotes the same values. By including steps to improve active de-escalation and your approach to sleep in your plan for professional growth, you endorse the use of time and space to develop a healthier balance needed to work at the outer limits of your abilities. You maintain your cognitive health because doing so has become expected of your development as a leader.

Prioritizing time for these steps lets you identify your ideal goal and the resulting efforts that can expand your capacity as a leader. Such effort would be highly personalized—everyone develops their own patterns and methods of coping. Each person brings different work environments and home environments to the effort, so their reactions need to be specific to their given circumstances. As you come to understand the nuances of your own circadian rhythm, areas of impact and focus will emerge. Some leaders may need to address wakefulness elements, sleep hygiene, or de-escalation—whatever is most appropriate to their given situation. As is the case with all parts of this book, the effort to build capacity is so deeply personalized that it must be developed by each individual.

Improve your sleep quality by examining your current sleep habits and making your environment as supportive as possible of sound sleep. The reproducible, "Sleep Hygiene Checklist" (page 102), invites you to take a closer look at your sleep environment and habits and reflect on what changes might bring about better sleep.

Bringing the Brain Back to Balance Using De-Escalation

While the sympathetic modifications to brain function provide a considerable advantage while in stressful situations, they also present a considerable challenge to your need to de-escalate and experience restorative sleep. Conversely, the parasympathetic nervous system is the body's way of slowing heart rate, redistributing blood flow to all areas of the body (digestion, reproduction, and immune systems), and bringing the brain back into a more sedate state. While this is a natural process, there are most definitely times when you need to help it along with some form of intentional support.

Much of the initial research in intentional de-escalation comes, once again, from the world of sports. For an athlete to perform at peak levels, they must be able to slow down their stress response in crucial moments of competition. Whether it's a basketball player trying to make a game-winning free throw, a golfer making a putt to win a tournament, or a jumper on their final attempt in the Olympic Games, it's not difficult to conjure up scenarios where overactive stress responses can work against a competitive athlete. Pulse rates rise, muscles tense, and the stomach feels like it's twisting into knots. The body is preparing to fight or flee—not to execute an intricate maneuver based on fine motor skills and focused concentration. In these circles, athletes are trained to slow the moment down and to prepare their body against their autonomic reaction. It begins with breathing.

Your nervous system, in all its intricacies, includes sensory neurons designed to sense feedback from your body. Among the most prominent of these sensory neurons is the vagus nerve. While there is no relation to the famous resort city in southern Nevada, the vagus nerve connects the brain to the organs in the chest and abdomen, providing feedback on their operation and condition. The vagus nerve is also responsible for adaptations associated with the parasympathetic nervous system. In other words, it's the mechanism by which the brain knows to slow things down after a stress activation. If you consciously alter your breathing patterns, the brain responds by slowing the heartbeat and other related responses (Breit, Kupferberg, Rogler, & Hasler, 2018). This is why so many relaxation techniques include intentional breathing patterns that empower you to exert control over our parasympathetic response. Relative to sleep, intentional use of de-escalation techniques, such as breath work and meditation, can help you return your mind to a state of being more suitable to sleep.

The intent of altered breathing techniques is to trigger the vagus nerve and, with it, the parasympathetic response. Slowing down exhalation to a point where it is considerably slower than inhalation signals the vagus nerve that the perceived threat has passed and it is time to slow the entire sympathetic activation (Gerritsen & Band, 2018). As a part of planning for capacity building, it is important to examine different tools like breath work or meditation strategies. It's worth noting, you are encouraged to stay open-minded to approaches that you may not have tried before or that you may not have had success with. For example, you may not have had a positive experience with meditation in the past, but there are many different techniques and tools that may work for you if you come at it with a curious and open mind. Guided meditation recordings or yoga nidra are two examples worth exploring, and there are many more. The key is to focus on your desired outcome.

Dealing With Fatigue

Most leaders acknowledge that they are not at their best when tired and in a depleted state. It's likely you have apologized for a moment of insensitivity or an ill-informed decision made in the fog of sleeplessness. While fatigue can be difficult to manage, the impact it has on a leader's day-to-day work makes it essential to address.

Begin with awareness and acknowledgment. If you are cognizant of your depleted state in the moment, you can accommodate for it in the way you interact with either the people you lead or those you serve. One short-term strategy might include using a *parachute phrase*, which is a predetermined phrase used to step away from an escalating situation to prevent a negative outcome. An example of a parachute phrase is, "I think it would be better to continue this discussion in my office." Another short-term strategy is to preemptively reschedule or relocate away from difficult situations when you know ahead of time that you are not at your best. In the long term, you can use good sleep hygiene and de-escalation strategies to avoid fatigue and revisit that situation in a less depleted state.

A wider acknowledgment of your efforts to build the leadership team's capacity sets a context for bridging short-term demands with longer-term efforts in this area. By building protocols or expectations for your interaction with others, you can navigate situations that might otherwise be awkward. You can recognize the impact your fatigue has, either on the decision at hand or on the dynamics of a situation, and accommodate accordingly.

To illustrate this approach, you might hypothetically consider a challenging meeting with a parent. As a leader in the school community committed to increasing capacity in decision making and communication, you recognize that your current state of mind may be compromised. Therefore, you invite a second member of your leadership team into the meeting to ensure meeting details are conveyed appropriately. You might also defer any potential decision or outcome of this meeting to allow for a secondary review or consideration of pertinent details. Ultimately, you factor in the possibility of a fatigued or stress-driven decision affecting the process, which is more possible in an environment that has already established the priority of leadership capacity and optimal functioning. Redundancy and time for review become an expectation instead of an in-the-moment reaction.

By establishing a value for optimal levels of functioning and permitting leaders to accommodate any self-perceived states of depletion, you create an environment where accurate self-perception is factored into the expectations of interactions. This accommodation is not seen as some sort of attempt to avoid responsibilities—instead, it acknowledges the importance of optimal performance.

Think of it this way. If an athlete in a competition realizes they are depleted enough that their state affects the optimal level of team performance, they are expected to step aside for a teammate who may be healthier or in some way better suited for that moment. In a process known among athletes as *tapping out*, from the widely used on-field sign of tapping oneself on the head to signify the need for a substitute, players are expected to self-identify when their performance is hindered by injury or fatigue. Their diminished performance affects the overall team function. The act requires self-awareness and value for the team's performance over one's own ego to realize that they aren't performing at their best and make the necessary accommodation for the greater good. The next chapter discusses leadership and emotional regulation.

Questions for Reflection

Use the following questions to help you reflect on what you have read in this chapter.

1. How much do you sleep on average on a night before work? Does your sleep pattern vary on work nights versus weekend nights?

2. How would you characterize the quality of your sleep? What elements do you think are important to you to obtain a quality night's sleep? What detracts from your sleep quality?

3. What strategies do you use to de-escalate after a stressful event? How do you relieve stress after either prolonged or repeated stress events over a week or over a month?

4. If given the time to do so, what strategy or activity would you like to learn more about that you believe would help you restore normal cognitive functioning after a prolonged or intense stressful situation?

5. What strategies do you employ when you recognize that your state of mind may inhibit your decision making in a stressful situation (for example, short sleep, illness, or activated stress response)? What other strategies might you use to accommodate these situations?

Sleep Hygiene Checklist

According to sleep expert Matthew Walker (2017), the following factors can support better sleep. Generally referred to as sleep hygiene, each of these habits also holds opportunities for closer examination should they indicate an area that is particularly difficult for you.

- ☐ Maintain a consistent bedtime and wake-up time.

- ☐ Aim for thirty minutes of daily exercise, but finish your workout at least three hours before bed.

- ☐ Avoid caffeine, nicotine, and alcohol.

- ☐ Avoid large meals or too much water near bedtime.

- ☐ Avoid naps after 3 p.m.

- ☐ Include time to wind down and relax without electronic devices an hour or so before bedtime.

- ☐ Take a hot bath or shower before bedtime.

- ☐ Keep your bedroom dark and free of electronic gadgets.

- ☐ Keep your bedroom cool. Your internal body temperature must drop one or two degrees to fall asleep.

- ☐ Get morning exposure to direct sun to help set your circadian rhythms.

- ☐ Don't lie awake in bed for longer than twenty to thirty minutes. If you can't fall asleep, get up and do something that is nonstimulating to help you feel tired and ready to sleep again (read dry material, create simple arts and crafts, work on a puzzle, and so on).

Reference

Walker, M. (2017). *Why we sleep: Unlocking the power of sleep and dreams*. New York: Scribner.

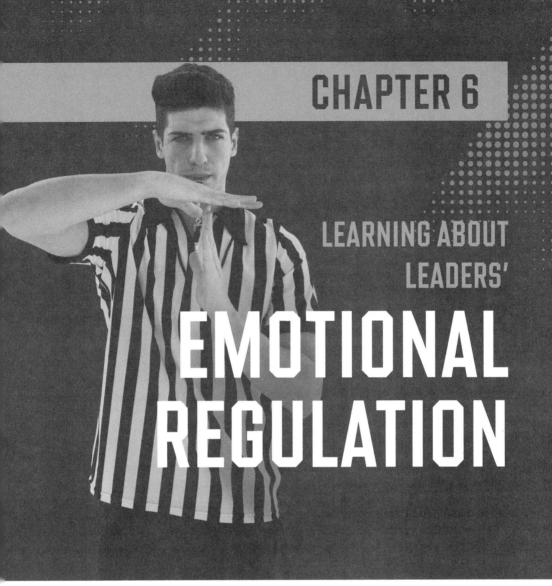

CHAPTER 6

LEARNING ABOUT LEADERS' EMOTIONAL REGULATION

Why Athletes Use Simulations and Mental Rehearsal

At times, it can feel like we are very much at the mercy of our emotions. They simply occur—at times to our benefit and others to our detriment. Most competition is emotionally charged. Participants are engaged in the flow of the event and deeply invested in the outcome. There is a constant flow of excitement—anticipation, elation, and disappointment all come and go throughout any competitive experience. How, then, do successful athletes learn to manage these conditions and thrive within them? The fundamental key lies in the concept of simulation.

In fast-paced competition, there is often little or no time to react in a reflective or analytical way. With so many subtle variables colliding at once, competitors must rely instead on advanced planning and preparation to react appropriately within the context of a game, match, or race. Such instantaneous adaptation can certainly bring elevated levels of anxiety as athletes try to slow down the game enough to react to changes. Simulation is one of the more common techniques that athletes use to reduce this anxiety and psychological stress. Simulations are used in advanced training to prepare for situational adaptations during competition. To facilitate this process, coaches and athletes turn to the if-then relationship.

By preparing in advance for potential adaptations (ifs), athletes give themselves the opportunity to focus on the more nuanced elements of preparation, such as tactical adjustments or physiological preparation (thens). "If something specific happens during a game, then I will . . . ." From an emotional standpoint, these if-then scenarios lessen the anxiety of adjusting to the unknown. While it's not possible to prepare for all possible adjustments, it is possible to address the most likely ones. This doesn't remove emotion, but it does remove the anxiety and confusion that can be magnified by the pace of competition.

As an example, consider a ski racer preparing for a giant slalom event. These races are decided by hundredths of a second, impacted by racers moving at speeds typical of cars on a highway. There is little time for reaction or adjustment; racers must make as many decisions as possible before they even board the lift to the mountaintop. Snow conditions can necessitate changes in ski tuning or waxing. A sunny day produces different snow conditions than a cloudy one, and the racers' position in the race order will determine the amount of snow that is skied off by the time they step into the starting gates. In each of these situations, racers prepare their approach and equipment well ahead of time, reducing pre-race anxiety. Racers also learn the slope and line of a course, as well as the gate positions, which allows them to mentally rehearse their run, sometimes hundreds of times, before they actually ski the race. In all situations, these preparations are framed in if-then language. For example, if the sun is out, then the racer adjusts accordingly. If they have a later start position, then they will change their run with course effects in mind. Knowing these adjustments ahead of time allows the racer to reduce their pre-race anxiety and realize the full benefits of a relaxed but focused approach to their preparation. The racer channels the excitement of the race into their performance instead of allowing their mind to overwork into full-blown anxiety.

This same type of simulation is applied to post-event debriefing by using video review to learn lessons in preparation for the next event. For example, many football teams review video recordings of each game on a highly detailed, play-by-play and player-by-player basis with the intent of discerning the reasons each play succeeded or failed. If-then thinking guides these mental simulations as well. If you use this tactic against this particular situation, then you have an increased likelihood of being successful. Using if-then allows for future planning, preparation, and tactical adjustments.

The work you do in leading schools is no less complex, nor is it less emotionally charged. By implementing opportunities to simulate emotionally charged situations and by debriefing them after they occur, you can reduce both the anticipation-based anxiety of these events and the resulting psychological stress escalation that inevitably follows. Again, you can't prepare for everything, but you can reduce the load of those things that you can anticipate. Contingency planning and preemptive thinking are often lost in the full schedule of your day—yet it could be one of the most useful tools you have to make them flow a little smoother.

The emotional demands of leading school systems or facilities are inherent in the complexities of the work. You are drawn to this work because you care about your learners and your staff, which alone is a source of anxiety. Beyond that, with all the personalities and competing priorities that you manage, you are entitled to your own emotional reactions. While attempts to balance these demands are a part of most leaders' roles, an active approach to building emotional support systems is often an afterthought. A comprehensive reconsideration of professional development for leaders includes an intentional structure of resources that provides appropriate emotional support for each leader in a manner consistent with their needs, role, circumstances, and resources available.

The need for emotional support systems is as varied as the leadership roles and those who work within them. That said, there are common needs that can be filled as a means of ensuring comprehensive support. They include personal emotional support, stress management resources, professional consultation and fellowship, and counseling for more complex challenges. This chapter discusses dealing with emotions in school, staying emotionally healthy, caring for social needs, and taking advantage of therapeutic support.

There are few substitutes for the value gained from developing school leaders' abilities to react well in emotionally charged moments. To supplement those experiences and accelerate professional learning, leaders turn to the same approach that is so typical in athletic training—mental rehearsal and simulation. The reproducible, "Using Mental Rehearsal and Simulation to Prepare for Escalated Emotional Response" (page 120), includes a structure that can help build simulations in a variety of professional learning experiences for school leaders.

Dealing With Emotions in School

Leadership in any context brings with it an environment that is ripe with emotional complications. You interact with people of all ages and stages in their careers throughout the day. These interactions present a variety of different windows for emotional experience, yet you may not be free to express your own emotions in an open and genuine manner. Leaders carry the responsibility for setting an emotional tone that is appropriate for the purposes of their respective organizations. This is particularly true in education. The tone you set must create an environment conducive to learning. A relaxed but productive mood comes to mind—one in which students can remain focused, teachers can apply their craft, and the overall operation of the school is as smooth and distraction free as possible.

District-level leadership is no less nuanced because leaders maintain the same mood among a wider variety of schools and constituents. It falls to leaders to take this multifaceted, busy environment and make it appear to run without complication—even when there are plenty of complications around. The world of education isn't exactly supportive of animated expressions of emotion, at least for those adults charged with operating it.

So, where do emotions come from, and how do they play into the larger picture of leadership capacity? This topic begins with a broader understanding of what emotions are and how they are generated. Lisa Feldman Barrett (2017a), a leading voice in the field of psychiatry and the study of emotion and the brain, describes in *How Emotions Are Made: The Secret Life of the Brain* the latest understanding of brain function and the way people experience emotions. She dives deep into how emotions serve multiple purposes for the brain and how they evolve over the course of a lifetime.

Barrett (2017a) sets forth the theory of *constructed emotion*, which is a process by which the brain compiles concepts or categories of experiences throughout a person's lifetime to assist them in predicting the outcomes of experiences before they happen. The brain anticipates the nature of these experiences and how the body needs to adapt to the energy demands of a given situation. It deploys information gathered from your interoceptive network—your internal means of monitoring energy needs and reactions (a connection to allostatic load)—in this process of anticipation. Given this complex process, the brain can then focus on input from the senses to either confirm these anticipatory simulations or adapt in the case of an error in anticipation.

The broader outcome of this process of anticipation and adaptation generates the reactions commonly known as emotions (Barrett, 2017a).

Some of the points to be gleaned here are that emotions are generated by the brain in an increasingly complex process, informed by life experiences and the culture or context in which you live. Your experiences build concepts and, from them, the simulations the brain produces. As such, you are not helpless to your emotions. As time passes and you gain more experience, the nature and degree of your emotional reactions change. That which was once an immediate source of fear in each situation may not remain so.

This speaks both of the value of experience and of an intentional and reflective approach to your work as a leader. The more experiences you have, the more comfortable you become with what may lie ahead. The more you can anticipate potential pitfalls, the less frightening these possibilities become. Experience and the ability to anticipate potential situations allow you to lessen the process of psychological stress activation and anxiety about what's coming next (Barrett, 2017a).

Everyone has strengths and weaknesses relative to how they handle emotionally charged situations. These compose your capacity to handle the variety of circumstances that are part of school leadership. Here again, Barrett's (2017a) work aids in understanding the broader matter of stress. In explaining the connection between the circumstances that surround you and the way your body reacts, she posits:

> You might think that stress is something that happens to you, like when you try to juggle five tasks at once, or that your boss tells you that tomorrow's work was due yesterday, or you lose a loved one. But stress doesn't come from the outside world. You construct it. (Barrett, 2017a, p. 203)

Barrett (2017a) elaborates, saying that, just like with the brain and what are known as conventional emotions, the body anticipates the outcomes of its surroundings and adjusts internal resources to match the expectation. The resulting emotional response becomes the way you perceive the stressfulness of a situation. This accounts for your sympathetic and parasympathetic responses and the resulting allostatic load. The result is a unique idea: Your physiological and emotional responses to stress are very subjective, just like the way you think about them. You generate emotional experiences by anticipating how those events will play out; from those emotions, you generate your responses.

Since so many of the emotional components of stress responses occur within the brain, is it possible that you have more control over your autonomic reactions than you might otherwise believe? If the stability of your stress response comes from your ability to simulate challenging incidents ahead of time, you could identify areas of your leadership responsibilities that cause you the greatest stress and deepen your preparation to reduce how much emotional stress you experience.

Simulation and mental rehearsal are both elements of preparing for competition and form the basis of most practice sessions or training exercises. Athletes experience simulations within the rehearsal elements of their training and while visualizing situations within future competitions. Live simulations are quite common, yet visualization is no less effective. In a literature review, researchers Fadare A. Stephen, Lambaco P. Ermalyn, Mangorsi B. Yasmin, Lorchano J. D. Louise, and Tercio B. Juvenmile (2022) examine the practice of visualization in sports and conclude:

> Visualizing has a significant impact on every athlete who wants to succeed in their various sports. It made a substantial contribution to the theoretical understanding of some mental processes explored in athletes' sports engagement during competition. It also demonstrates that the most effective visualization techniques should result in an incredibly vivid sports experience in which the athlete has entire control overachieving achievement. (p. 108)

In the workplace, how might simulations help you prepare for challenges and lower your arousal level ahead of them? Consider how some elements of school leadership prominently feature contingency planning, such as emergency operations planning, budgetary planning, program development planning, or even long-range strategic planning. Each of these processes involves advanced preparation for circumstances that can be anticipated and, as a result, leaders will be more readily able to accommodate those circumstances.

In practice, this concept would take the form of structured simulations of challenging leadership situations. School leaders might engage in role-playing exercises during which they handle challenging disciplinary situations with students, complicated circumstances with staff members, or even confrontational exchanges with parents or community members. If paired with an appropriate element of instruction and review regarding the experience, such activities could equip school leaders with the means to handle emotionally charged situations with greater confidence and lessened anxiety. Even if facilitated without actual live-performance elements of simulation, school leaders would reap the benefits of visualizing and mentally rehearsing these interactions with the benefits of planning and debriefing to bracket the experiences.

You have only begun to leverage the concept of advanced planning and simulation as a means of lowering stress responses. By simulating events that school leaders find to be the most stressful, they can be equipped with the necessary cognitive concepts to be able to engage in those issues when they do encounter them in their work. This makes the situation less stressful and the leader more effective within it.

Staying Emotionally Healthy

School and district leaders are people too. Yes, the demands of the work are such that they might make sacrifices that affect their well-being in the interest of doing their jobs well. What about the impact these sacrifices have on the capacity to lead, though? When you can function as a self-actualized and emotionally regulated person, you walk within the scope of your work fully aware of your surroundings, able to adapt to changes as they arise, and capable of interacting with a wide variety of people who may be experiencing an array of emotions themselves. Each of these components helps you function within the complex role of leadership. Your emotional state becomes an asset to the work rather than a complication.

Building a version of yourself that is self-actualized and emotionally regulated requires you to understand the components of emotional health and how to apply them to the leadership environment. Common fundamental components of emotional health from a variety of experts include the following.

- **Self-awareness:** You maintain the ability to know yourself as objectively as possible, both within your job responsibilities and in the wider context of your life (Landry, 2019).
- **Coping skills, self-management, and regulation:** Often, the leadership role demands that you react to emotional situations in a calm and rational way. You can engage in emotionally challenging situations and maintain your composure, as well as an appropriate decorum and demeanor as required by each given situation (Landry, 2019).
- **Emotional adaptability:** You can participate in a variety of different emotional circumstances while maintaining a productive role in the situation. You make difficult matters better (Utecht, 2023).
- **Social skills, empathy, and awareness of others:** You can read the emotional content of a situation to understand the perspectives of others within it, to diagnose the most appropriate way to engage it,

and to conclude it with sensitivity to all participants (Brower, 2022; National Health Service, 2022).

These qualities are not exhaustive but represent an overview of a healthy emotional perspective for a leader. There are as many wide-ranging definitions of emotional needs for adults as there are researchers to compile them. This chapter looks to assemble these common elements to inform planning efforts for personal emotional well-being as a component of your leadership capacity.

Self-Management and Regulation

First and foremost, leaders are human beings. They interact with their respective worlds, and their emotional states are affected by those interactions. Because how you express your emotions can impact your capacity to lead, it becomes more important that you maintain an awareness of how you are projecting emotions, manage how you regulate your behavior, and manage how you cope with the outcomes of your own emotional trials. You are not exempt from life's emotional challenges.

Leaders have undoubtedly been in situations where they are faced with some form of emotional crisis outside of work, or for some reason, they are distracted and feeling less emotionally engaged. They find themselves challenged to bring the level of presence and awareness that the job requires. Then, they walk through the door to school, and find people who still need them. Those people are looking to leaders to provide the attention and empathy they need to teach or learn that day. Conscientious leaders rise to the moment. They deliver what is needed, even though doing so might require them to fake that level of outward engagement. This is not a disingenuous moment—it is a demonstration of the selfless priorities required to lead a school or district. Leaders do so with a sense of care and professional obligation. They set aside their own frame of mind in favor of the needs of others. It's part of leading in schools—however, making a habit of the practice can wear you thin over time. There is a time for self-management and regulation, and there is a time when things have gone too far. This is when it is time to step away and seek support.

Leadership teaches about the added level of responsibility you carry relative to expressing your own emotions. Through your affect, you set the tone in your working environment. For better or for worse, those you lead will take cues from how you handle both positive and negative circumstances, and often the reaction that you are expected to give will not match the one you would like to express. You are held to a different standard when it comes to emotional regulation, and appropriately so. Leaders have a tremendous impact on the mood of the building where they serve.

For example, consider a moment of frustration. You encounter a student who is in crisis and is clearly in need of significant support, either from the school staff or from outside agencies. You may not be able to access the kind of support you believe the student needs, and your frustration may manifest itself in the form of thoughts, expressions, or words that display you aren't happy. You know that the way you interact with others who may be able to provide the needed support could determine a different direction in the situation, and that raising your voice or making negative comments could only hurt the situation. Therefore, you anticipate the potential impact of a forthright expression of frustration and choose to stifle it in favor of another approach. In this situation, you put forth a reaction that favors a more appropriate outcome instead of one that allows you to vent your frustration.

While this is a hypothetical example, it isn't difficult for leaders to recall other similar experiences. Leaders' need for emotional expression is stifled in the best interest of the organization or the people within it. Leaders come to understand that, by the way they regulate and communicate emotional reactions, they affect the tone of the organization around them.

Of course, there are times when leaders can express genuine or negative emotions, even if that expression creates tension. You learn, through experiences, to judge the circumstances in a moment, and to moderate how you express yourself to meet the needs of those you lead. There is substantial research that supports the importance of emotional expression to our overall health. One such source states, "it is clear that expressing one's true emotions and the feeling is crucial to physical health, mental health, and general well-being, while a reliance on concealment gives rise to a barrier to good health" (Patel & Patel, 2019, p. 20). Regulating our emotions in certain situations is necessary, though a pattern of repression is another matter.

But what does that do to you? It is only through maintaining self-awareness and an ongoing understanding of your health that you can know when the load has become too heavy. There is a time when you should put aside the brave face and seek out more formal, professional support to maintain your emotional health. Too often, this step is postponed or ignored to your detriment. By compromising on the support you need in favor of busy schedules or appearances, you enter your work each day in a state of reduced capacity.

There is a difference between a leader exhibiting mental strength or perseverance and modeling a healthy practice of reaching out for help. By maintaining a healthy mindset relative to seeking support when needed, you can both preserve your own capacity and be a role model for the others you lead in doing the same.

This is the point where self-regulation and coping skills become a matter of practice. Those you lead certainly look to you in times of emotional challenge and appreciate your strength, but they also stand to benefit from your example in times where the burden gets too heavy. Whether by seeking support from a counselor, stepping away from your role temporarily to address a personal crisis, or restructuring your responsibilities in the short term to create emotional respite, you have an opportunity to model appropriate coping skills and a value for emotional balance. Naturally, few leaders would take such actions either lightly or regularly, but doing so when appropriate can be a positive leadership example.

Emotional Adaptability

The sheer breadth of emotional situations that confront a school or district leader over the course of a given day can be dizzying. Students across K–12 are growing and developing in complex social environments that they don't always know how to navigate. Leaders guide staff members who bring their own emotional experiences to work each day. They encounter both parents and community members in circumstances related to their children or to the context of schooling, each of which brings its own set of emotional reactions. In their midst, leaders stand as those responsible for maintaining a climate that is conducive to learning. It is little wonder that the ability to adapt to a variety of emotional circumstances is such a valuable trait for school leaders.

And it is valuable. So long as they are responsible for a school's climate, it will be crucial for them to react appropriately to emotionally charged situations. The connection to self-management is evident—leaders project the reaction that is most beneficial given the circumstances. It is outward facing in a moment, and yet emotional adaptability goes deeper.

To remain healthy in this regard, turn this same concept inward by establishing a means of working through challenging emotional circumstances not only by behaving appropriately, but also by managing your own emotional reactions before, during, and after an incident. You attend to your own inward emotions in anticipation of the challenges you face, and to support your larger emotional well-being on an ongoing basis. While leaders are expected to moderate their behavior, they also benefit from an ability to adapt internally. The resulting behaviors include the ability to embrace challenges and adapt to them in real time in a manner that expands the work of their organization (Utecht, 2023).

In practice, emotional adaptability is rooted in our ability to see both the underlying issues in a charged situation and the most appropriate means of navigating a proactive outcome. Take, for example, a complex disciplinary situation. Say that a student is sent to the office after repeatedly falling asleep in class and arguing with the teacher about their inattentiveness. The teacher is agitated, and the student reacts with inappropriate language. As you address the situation, you might be quick to engage with the student to quell their outburst. However, given a brief opportunity to decompress, you learn that the student is working a full-time job in the evening and often arrives at school on little sleep and without breakfast. Here, your ability to adapt your approach quickly and focus on the core issue that precipitated the incident can mean the difference between handling this situation as a simple disciplinary measure or seeing it as a matter of student well-being. Your quick adaptation and emotional regulation provide an outcome that can resolve the matter and impact the likelihood of it recurring.

Remaining emotionally adaptable involves retaining the ability to encounter emotionally charged situations, both internally and externally, in a way that advances the requirements of your role. Yes, these experiences can be challenging, but they cause you to elevate your performance while remaining a calming influence among those you lead.

Social Skills, Empathy, and Awareness of Others

One of the most important and nuanced skills demanded of leaders in an environment as complex as a school is the ability to read the emotional content of a situation in a moment and to react appropriately. Students and staff alike bring the weight of their individual worlds into the halls each day, and it falls to school leaders to maintain a safe and productive learning environment amid the outcome. Just as the previous section details the importance of being able to adapt your emotional response, it is logical that much of your work subsequent to that response revolves around your ability to read the emotional content of a situation, understand the perspectives of others within it, diagnose the most appropriate way to engage it, and conclude it with sensitivity to all participants in the situation. This is no small task, and it certainly doesn't come naturally to everyone. Thus, it is so important to remain cognizant of your own emotional awareness while working at the outer limits of your capacity.

Empathy and the skills to bring it to life are widely recognized as fundamental elements of effective leadership in any environment. "Great leadership requires a fine mix of all kinds of skills to create the conditions for engagement, happiness and performance, and empathy tops the list of what leaders must get right" (Brower, 2022). If a leader's ultimate responsibility is to inspire those they lead toward a desired outcome, maintaining awareness of and accommodating for their emotional states become a central element.

So, what is the best way to demonstrate empathy and the social skills to adapt to emotional context? The good news is that it's not as complicated as it might appear. Sociologist and author Tracy Brower (2022) continues, "Leaders don't have to be experts in mental health in order to demonstrate they care and are paying attention. It's enough to check in, ask questions and take cues from the employee about how much they want to share." In other words, a little goes a long way. By remaining aware of the importance of demonstrating empathy and practicing basic social skills in relation to emotionally charged situations on a consistent basis, you can maintain an environment that is both supportive and engaging. Just remember that your staff are watching—an environment is created by consistent action, not by one moment. Emotional awareness, therefore, must become a part of daily life in your school.

The reproducible, "Maintaining Emotional Supports Graphic Organizer" (page 122), walks you through a structured framework to develop a plan for your emotional support across a school year. It asks that you consider both ongoing support and contingency plans for significant events that you could encounter over a given year.

Social Needs

The social and emotional needs of a person in a leadership role do not change just because they are in a leadership role. You remain human first and foremost, and with that, you are subject to the positive and negative influences of emotional health.

To start with a foundational concept of psychology, Abraham H. Maslow's (1943) hierarchy of needs places belonging right after safety. Unfortunately, needs like belonging or respect from others are routinely sacrificed to the demands of the work, yet they are needs that people still have. You're aware of meeting needs relative to students in crisis, for staff members, or for the commitment of program resources. But you often don't consider the manner in which these needs fit with your own day-to-day experiences. Yes, you are also in need of fulfillment, and often your emotional well-being is reliant on it.

Take the need for belonging as an example. One key element to emotional well-being is the presence of a support network. Humans are social creatures—you need other people to feel validated, as a source of acceptance and support, and with whom to share your experiences and challenges. The need for belonging is wired into human nature. Unfortunately, in the full days and weeks of many school leaders, friendships are often sacrificed or at least de-emphasized. It is assumed that, by virtue of their position, leaders simply have less access to social time or a forum to fulfill their need for a sense of belonging. Often, they become so identified with their roles that, when leaders do reach out to clubs, activities, or sports for a sense of community and belonging, they are still regarded in a different manner because they are the principal or the superintendent in the local school district.

Given the fullness of their lives at work and the scarcity of time beyond it, leaders often look to work relationships to fill social needs. This is complicated by leadership roles—colleagues, more specifically those whom you supervise, are not social friends. Work requires school leaders to maintain an appropriate social distance out of a need for objectivity. Leaders can't be too friendly with their colleagues because they must maintain the ability to act as their boss when needed. Leaders may look here to fulfill their need for socialization, but their colleagues are not their friends.

So, who are your friends then? Your work fills most of your day, but those people you spend that time with are not appropriate people to fill your need for socialization. Social time goes unfilled, and with it your clearly articulated need for socialization. Something has to give.

Again, this is an odd situation that has little to do with a conventional program of professional development, yet you can easily draw a line to the lack of human fulfillment potentially impacting your well-being—and ultimately affecting your ability to work at optimal levels of professional capacity. It seems to be a stretch to think that a need for socialization is an appropriate component for a professional development plan, particularly for a person who does not have any such source in their life. Even so, loneliness does impact your capacity to lead. If you are to bring a sense of fulfillment to your work, you must attend to your own needs to be healthy.

By acknowledging the basic human needs that you bring to your experiences, you give yourself the chance to live a healthier and fuller emotional life, and to bring a deeper sense of strength and stability to the challenges of your work. You prioritize your emotional needs not to be selfish, but to be more fully engaged. Therefore, it becomes a foundational element of your capacity to build in opportunities—where appropriate—for you to experience social connections outside of your work life. Of course, this is highly subjective and should be planned by individual leaders in a manner that best meets their needs. But it does need to happen.

Taking Advantage of Therapeutic Support

A separate source of emotional support, even if entered into reluctantly, can provide leaders with a non-judgmental and professional source of insight and self-care. Many leaders approach their work from both an exaggerated degree of commitment and a selfless perspective, resulting in either a reluctance to seek formal therapies or a lack of awareness that they even need to seek it. How can you know when it is time to turn your attention to outside support? You may have to rely on others to help you determine that.

First, engaging in any form of therapy is not a sign of weakness in a leader. It is a sign of self-awareness and a commitment to well-being resulting in your ability to work at the outer limits of your capacity. You expect such things from your teams and families—why are you exempt from seeking out therapeutic support? You become both a stronger leader and a positive role model to those you lead if you can recognize this need and are willing to seek it out. You display your strength not by ignoring your needs, but by recognizing and acting on them.

Here is another example from the world of competitive sports. An athlete can force themselves to remain in competition despite an injury that may be affecting their level of performance. In their mind, they may be making a sacrifice for the benefit of their team—but in truth, the injury may lower their level of performance to a point where the team may benefit from them stepping away and allowing a teammate to take on their responsibilities. In the long term, that athlete may provide a greater service to their team by stepping away and gaining the formal support available to them, resulting in a comprehensive recovery from the injury and a return to full performance levels.

It's the same for leaders. Often, you resist seeking out formal therapeutic support out of either resistance or lack of awareness, yet that therapy may be the one thing that will help you return to full capacity. By recognizing the significance of that support in restoring your work to more optimum performance levels, you are prioritizing both the organization you lead and your own health and well-being.

Just what kind of support should you consider? There are many different forms of emotional supports and therapies available to you, varied by what you need and the resources available to you from both your respective employers and the communities where you serve.

The following are a few that may help school leaders in times of struggle.

- **Individual therapy:** This type of support can assist with traumatic experiences or personal struggles. These resources feature more personalized and private support given the nature of the need. It is also not uncommon for leaders to engage in regular, ongoing individual therapy to support the many challenges in their work (Palagi, 2024). Many therapies are also included as benefits under health insurance coverage.
  - Examples may include counseling for trauma, anxiety, depression, or grief.
- **Group therapy:** There are some challenges that are best supported through membership in a group of people experiencing similar challenges. Leaders are not exempt from needing such resources (Palagi, 2024). Many health insurance providers cover a portion or all costs for participation in groups as well.
  - Examples may include treatment programs or support for alcoholism or drug addiction, children of abuse or neglect, or grief support.
- **Associations or professional affiliations:** Many of these groups offer support to identified subgroups of membership. If the concept of capacity is fundamental to optimal performance, it stands to reason that such groups might offer emotional support resources from peers as well.
  - Examples may include state or regional professional associations; formal support around specific challenges, such as new principal or superintendent groups; or internal subgroups within the profession (for example, new leaders or members of a subgroup of leaders).
- **Resources available through employee services:** Health insurance programming or employee support systems offered by human resources departments are included in this category. Many of these resources go largely unused because of a lack of awareness or fear of how an employer or colleagues would perceive an employee who uses these services.
  - Examples may include employee assistance programs offered through school district human resources departments, wellness resources offered by health

insurance providers, or similar programming offered through state associations.

You are better able to access resources when you know what is offered and by whom. You need not become an expert in these programs, though it is well worth the time to know what is offered where, and how best to find out more information about them given a moment of need. In this sense, an abundance of awareness is as beneficial as a healthy reduction in personal pride.

Here again, the matter of public perception comes about. Some leaders still carry a concern about being seen at a support group meeting or entering a mental health professional's office. But seeking out professional help for support during a life crisis is not a sign of weakness or diminished ability. If you embrace the concept that, for you to perform at optimal levels within your work responsibilities, you must pursue balance in all areas of your life that impact that performance, you can no longer afford to allow variables limiting that performance to go unaddressed. You seek this level of support as a way of increasing your effectiveness and capacity.

Accessing more formal programs or resources for emotional support is not a sign of weakness for leaders. Instead, it provides a positive example to your community members who may also be in need. Leaders are human beings and will encounter challenges during their lives. Reaching out to support resources when needed sends a message to the community that emotional well-being is fundamental for fulfilled living and is a core component of working at the outer limits of your capacity. The next chapter will explore motivation and volition.

Questions for Reflection

Use the following questions to help you reflect on what you have read in this chapter.

1. In general, how would you characterize your current state of emotional well-being? What factors might cause this characterization to change, either for better or for worse?

2. What supports do you use during emotional challenges within your job responsibilities? Are these different from those in your personal life?

3. What resources, such as counseling or employee assistance, are available through your workplace? Who might you talk to if you were experiencing emotional difficulties that affected your capacity to work?

4. What outside resources or organizations could provide you with support, even during your regular work and the emotional challenges that come with it?

5. In what ways do you make room for your own needs for socialization, belonging, or engagement beyond the scope of your work role? How might you seek out opportunities to maintain an identity beyond that of a school leader?

Using Mental Rehearsal and Simulation to Prepare for Escalated Emotional Response

The theory of constructed emotion states that most emotional experiences are a product of anticipated or simulated thought (Barrett, 2017a). Therefore, how might you use this to your advantage by including opportunities to simulate emotionally charged experiences for school leaders well ahead of their occurrences? As with emergency response planning and the use of table-top drills, you can apply simulation training to leaders' professional development experience. Establishing simulated responses in practice can help them avoid the anxiety of the unknown elements. This simple practice can readily be incorporated into regular professional development sessions within a school or district.

A few potential areas for simulation might include the following.

- Challenging student disciplinary situations

- Emotionally charged interactions with parents or colleagues

- Responding to questions regarding procedure or student and staff handbooks

- Responding to community members regarding an academic initiative

- Addressing controversial issues within a school cocurricular program

Structuring a Simulation: A Protocol

The following structure may be applied to the process of creating a training simulation for school leaders. This simulation allows for more efficient application of the training approach.

1. **Focus of interaction:** Student, parent, staff member, and so on

2. **Content matter:** School policy, disciplinary matter, and so on

3. **Simulation details:** Time, place, duration, persons involved, and so on

4. **Professional competencies under consideration:** Effective communication, conflict resolution, policy interpretation, and so on

5. **Set the scene:** Brief paragraph outlining the people involved in the simulation and the roles they will play, the matter to be addressed, support resources in place, and norms for the exercise or rules by which participants will adhere

6. **Facilitator:** The only team member who will step outside the simulation, enforce norms, and keep time and task

The simulation will be carried out in table-top fashion with members playing their given roles without physical movement or interaction. The duration will change according to the requirements of the topic and the participants involved. The facilitator will monitor time and will declare either a resolution or an impasse as the simulation comes to the end of its course or time limit.

Reference

Barrett, L. F. (2017a). *How emotions are made: The secret life of the brain.* Boston: Houghton Mifflin Harcourt.

Maintaining Emotional Supports Graphic Organizer

Use this planning tool as a yearlong reference for maintaining emotional supports.

1. **Time frames for check-ins:** Add dates for prescheduled opportunities to check on the state of your emotional well-being and potential need for supports.

    - Summer planning: _____ / _____ / _____

    - Interval 1: _____ / _____ / _____

    - Interval 2: _____ / _____ / _____

    - Interval 3: _____ / _____ / _____

    - Year-end debrief: _____ / _____ / _____

2. **Topics of focus:** Review possible emotional supports.

    - What sources of emotional support would be the most meaningful and authentic for you to include in this plan?

3. **Modes of reflection:** What format will you use to document and monitor your emotional well-being and potential sources of support?

    - Written (journaling, calendar notations, or correspondence)
    - Verbal (consultation with peers, as either individuals or groups)
    - Intrapersonal (retreat and reflect)
    - Other modes:

4. **Intervention strategies:** Who will you contact when a crisis arises? Please list all resources available to you and note those with specific areas of focus.

    - Personal matters (non-work related):

- Work-related resources:

- Family support:

- Other important sources of support:

5. **Resources to research:** What resources are missing from your list of available emotional supports? How can you add to these resources?

    - Formal therapeutic support:

    - Professional consultation:

    - Mentorship support:

    - Other:

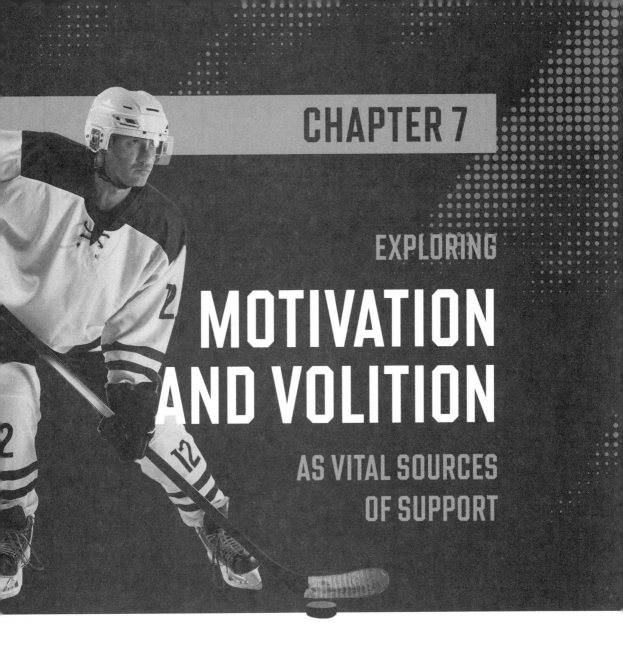

CHAPTER 7

EXPLORING MOTIVATION AND VOLITION AS VITAL SOURCES OF SUPPORT

Athletes Connect to What Motivates Them

Motivation is inherent in competitive sports. Athletes must be motivated to train and compete. As is the case with school leaders, many athletes are motivated to show up to train each day and to make the sacrifices necessary to engage in competition. The work is intense, the hours are grueling, and the promise of success is often remote. Why do they work so hard and pay so dearly for uncertain athletic pursuits? So many athletes chase their dreams and have a complicated relationship with their sense of motivation. The problem arises when either they just aren't sure why they do it or, worse yet, the reasons that move them to compete aren't fulfilling. It's less a matter of being motivated than being fulfilled by that which motivates them.

Consider the path of an Olympic hockey player. The sport begins with children as young as three or four years old learning to skate. Because rinks are in short supply, time on ice is at a premium, and practices are often held in the predawn hours or later at night. Hockey players grow up in this environment. Travel teams begin competition when players are very young, and they often require national or international travel. The sport is extremely demanding physically, the gear is cumbersome and expensive, competition for spots on teams becomes intense as players get older, and the likelihood of progressing to the Olympic level is remote. After all, the men's and women's U.S. Olympic hockey teams have only twenty-five spots each, with hundreds of thousands of young players dreaming for a spot. So, how does a thirteen-year-old force themselves to get up and go to a 4 a.m. hockey practice or spend their holidays traveling to remote tournaments? What keeps them going? Each athlete remembers the source of their motivation in those moments.

This is yet another entry point as you investigate the elements of leadership capacity. Like athletes, leaders are committed to their work and dive in each day, driven by the variety of expectations necessary to lead schools. An awareness of what motivates them provides the fuel needed to power through the difficulties inherent in that world.

Conversely, if the source of their motivation changes or is no longer enough to provide that fuel, disillusionment isn't far away. One example might be the power of approval from peers or family. This can drive some athletes to achieve, and yet there are points where the strength of that drive may wane as the athlete realizes such approval. They may find that recognition or affirmation that comes with sports may no longer be sufficient to fulfill them. There are many reasons to pursue athletic achievement, and all are deeply personal. In the end, awareness of that driving force allows them to remain connected to and motivated by an idea as circumstances push them to their limits.

The connection here is a natural one. The work of a school leader is difficult. Your job is complex and requires considerable sacrifice. If you are unsure of why you do what you do or if the reasons why are not sufficient to power you through the inevitable adversity, you will find yourself lost and unfulfilled. By maintaining an awareness of the source of your motivation, you give yourself a chance to connect the day-to-day work you do to a larger sense of purpose. You are motivated by the power of an idea.

So often the concept of motivation is taken for granted. You know that there are factors that drive you, yet you give little value to the process of identifying and remaining aware of what those factors are or how they are affected by your choices and the environment. After all, motivation may not be something you experience in a conscious way. At face value, you may simply feel motivated or not. Without a clear awareness of your motivation, you might quickly find yourself wandering, void of fulfillment or purpose.

The process of burnout and loss of motivation to lead is no simple matter as seen throughout this book and the lived experiences of many school leaders. It stands to reason, then, that any attempt to preserve your motivation is likewise complicated. Thus far, this book has examined physical, cognitive, and emotional elements of your stressful work as a means of carving a path forward. This chapter will take a specific look at the roots of motivation. Maintaining an active and intentional awareness of the values that form the root cause of what drives you is key to maintaining your performance at optimal levels. This chapter explores ways leaders can do just that within the practical constraints of their work. First, it discusses how to realize your motivation and purpose and how to locate your volition. Next, it explores spirituality as an element of volition and why authentic reflection is essential. Last, it explains why it is important to surround yourself with your why.

Realizing Your Motivation and Purpose

Start by thinking of your worst days—the ugly days that leave you depleted and empty. On the worst of these, you might not even be sure you want to get up the next morning and go to work. Even if these feelings aren't chronic, you've no doubt experienced them at some point. Nearly all of those who do this work long enough do. During these moments, the primary question is typically, "Why do I do this?" You need to know why you should choose to continue.

Delving into a topic like motivation and volition seems to be a departure from the more practical experiences that make up the rest of this book. The cumulative impact of the physical demands, the cognitive strain, and the brand of emotional depletion that comes of school leaders' work sets the conditions for a deeper questioning of why you chose this career path. You are exhausted and depleted. Why continue? Even so, during those darker moments of life or leadership, most leaders still have the concepts and values that led them to this work in the first place that keep them going. The answer to "Why do I do this?" lies in your core concepts about what student learning should look like and your personal values that guide all the decisions you make each day. You do what you do because these larger forces support you. When life gets busy and challenging, you forget those forces at your own peril. Maintaining some form of authentic awareness of those concepts and values that motivate you allows you to persevere in the face of what often feels overwhelming.

In this context, the term *volition* refers to the root cause of motivation because it is the power and ability to make your own decisions. Volition tips the balance of the decisions made each day, both in the minute and on the grand scale. For most people, this is something that rarely moves to the level of awareness. However, awareness of what motivates you becomes a valuable tool by which you can sustain yourself through the inevitable challenges of your work. Remembering that you have the power and ability to make your own decisions powers you through.

Therefore, volition is at the heart of each day for leaders—you choose to lead at the outset. In the minutes and years that follow, leadership practice becomes a string of such choices within your work. No one is forced to take on a leadership position, nor is anyone obligated to lead in a situational sense. You choose to step up, and there is always a reason why you do. While there are many different contexts for leadership, it is defined, for this purpose, as being the intersection of two elements: (1) the acceptance of responsibility for a specific outcome and (2) a context of influence over others' participation in that process. You are in charge of making something happen, and that task involves you influencing others to help. In almost any context, the initial driver for a person to enter a leadership role is a choice to do so. Even in seemingly mandatory situations, a person must still choose to lead and then continue to do so.

Given that level of awareness regarding the roots of your choice to lead, you next acknowledge the two fundamental contexts that bring about the opportunity to lead in the first place: (1) positional leadership and (2) situational leadership. In *positional leadership*, you are hired to do a specific job that entails responsibility and influence. You receive a title and the responsibilities associated with it. In *situational leadership*, you find yourself in circumstances in which leadership is required, and you have some form of skill or knowledge that is needed to navigate it. In this form of leadership, you may not have the job title, but you find yourself in a situation where others look to you because of who you are. Both contexts require the person involved to choose to lead, even if in different ways. So, why would you say yes?

Indeed, *why* is central to understanding motivation in the larger sense, specifically in leadership. In *Start With Why: How Great Leaders Inspire Everyone to Take Action*, Simon Sinek (2009) dives deep into the benefits you gain from being aware of your sense of purpose as the root cause of your motivation. Sinek (2009) advocates for leaders to root their organizations in their *why* at the outset, with further elaboration in *how* and *what* they do from that point. Conventional organizational leadership, Sinek (2009) asserts, travels in the other direction by starting with what an organization does, how it does it, and ultimately to why as a potential afterthought (if at all).

While Sinek (2009) writes—at least in the initial concept—about the foundations of a company, the crucial nature of a sense of purpose as the root cause of motivation extends well beyond corporate success in the marketplace. Awareness of and adherence to a sense of purpose is also a fundamental element of individual motivation. People are better equipped to choose wisely when their choices are based on a deeper cause (Sinek, 2009).

Sinek (2009) points out that, in searching for the origins of your own sense of why (your purpose), you must begin by looking backward into your own history. He reminds you that, in many instances, the origins of motivation live in the earlier moments of your story. By understanding the formative events, trials, or values of your life, you can find core components of your own volition. There is always a reason why people are motivated by certain things, and frequently those reasons are developed during formative moments. As life progresses and becomes busier, you move on from those moments. Their impact remains, but your awareness of them fades. It is in this process that you lose awareness of what ultimately drives you.

If you extend the concept of volition as the point of decision at which you take action either to lead or to accept a leadership role, then you find, at the heart of those substantive moments, an equation that determines why you do what you do. In both a conscious and subconscious manner, you tally the variables involved in a choice, and the outcome sets your direction. At the heart of this equation, you prioritize the root cause of your motivation. Your why is literally the foundation of your decisions.

So then, how do you best give form to something as abstract as volition? Beyond a value for it, space to find it, and how to maintain awareness of it, there waits the challenge of giving form to this concept.

As a starting point for reflecting on the source of your motivation to lead, look at the different commonalities between what drives you. For this purpose, focus on three significant factors that define the scope of your source of motivation.

1. **Intrinsic versus extrinsic motivation:** Some people are motivated by values or rewards that they experience within their own minds (*intrinsic*), while others are driven more by factors existing in the world outside of them (*extrinsic*). The source of drive comes from the location of the reward. Intrinsic motivation results in an internal sense of accomplishment or fulfillment, regardless of the nature of the outcome that is visible in the world around you. This form of motivation is measured by the value created within the mind by experience. Extrinsic motivation is much more tangible. Results are external; they can be seen or measured by others.

2. **Aspirational versus historical motivation:** This variable is determined by which direction you look for inspiration. You can look to the past in search of inspiration, focusing on factors that have influenced your journey to your current leadership experience. You can be inspired by the prospects of either recreating these factors or building on them. Aspirational motivation, on the other hand, involves looking ahead to an experience you have not had yet, and you work to create it. In this case, you are motivated by an idea that is valuable to you and that you perceive as attainable.

3. **Positive versus negative motivation:** This is the classic variable of pursuing something out of a love for that experience versus an aversion to something or a desire for retribution for some past wrong. Positive motivation is forward looking. You do what you do because you enjoy it, you value the experiences and outcomes, and you derive a sense of fulfillment from it. Negative motivation is backward facing. What drives you exists in the past and propels you forward in search of some better future. This can be a very strong form of motivation, but it is very difficult to experience a sense of fulfillment. Those elements of the past that motivated you simply won't change, and any sense of closure is generated internally.

None of these motivations are exclusive in and of themselves—they are interconnected. By reflecting on these factors as sources of your volition, you are more able to define the roots of your motivation in more tangible ways. You know why you make the choices you do, and you can remain aware of and connected to it as you work through the daily challenges of leading schools.

Given these three factors and how they influence why you lose touch with your volition only serves to help you find it—where it lives and how you can maintain your awareness of it. You begin by applying a structure to the possible sources of that which motivates you.

The reproducible, "Uncovering Your Volition" (page 142), is a structured approach to reflecting on the significant decisions that you have made during your career progression. The series of questions focuses on different waypoints in the work of school leaders, pointing you toward some of the fundamental reasons behind your choice to lead.

Locating Your Motivation

Determining a location for your motivation is the first step in understanding it, and thus maintaining it. You are intrinsically motivated by concepts and values that propel you to act, therefore becoming a part of your volition. You make choices based on concepts such as fairness or validation. On the other hand, extrinsic motivation is just as it sounds—inspiration that comes from the outside world. In this sense, you are motivated by things like acquiring material possessions or providing for your family. You espouse these designations with your students, and yet they are universal to human behavior—and certainly to you as you try to clarify your own sources of motivation.

Differentiating intrinsic versus extrinsic motivation is a starting point. There is much more to the roots of human behavior, though. By contextualizing your motivation within the scopes of past versus future and positive versus negative, you can further connect with why you choose to do this work.

Figure 7.1 looks at the aspirational, historical, and positive and negative motivation summed up in two fundamental continua. The idea here is to generate a deeper look at what motivates you and where it comes from. By applying these concepts, you can peer into your own stories and identify pertinent formative experiences and how they have shaped you.

Locating Your Motivation: Where do you find the concepts and values that motivate you to lead?

	Past Memories	Future Expectations
Positive Orientation	**Happiness** Desire to replicate positive experiences	**Love** Aspire to create positive outcomes
Negative Orientation	**Anger** Need to compensate for adverse experiences	**Fear** Need to avoid adverse outcomes

FIGURE 7.1: Motivation source chart.

As you look at sources of motivation, look either to the past or to the future and attach them either to positive factors or to negative ones. It is in the combination of these elements that you find a clearer image of the source of your motivation. In this concept, you see the interrelation of these different factors. The following examines each window individually, allowing the foundational concepts to emerge.

1. **Positive orientation to past memories:** Here, you remember fondly either experiences or themes from your past that form pleasant memories. As such, you connect with the concepts resulting from these memories and are driven to recreate or perpetuate them.
   - *Example*—You fondly remember your childhood family vacations and are compelled to earn enough money to be able to recreate similar experiences for your own family. You extend this value to create similar opportunities for your students.

2. **Positive orientation to future expectations:** In this situation, you ground your motivation in aspiration. You form a picture of things that you are driven to create. This type of motivation is grounded in some form of value you bring to the experience, and your desire becomes to bring it into being.
   - *Example*—Over your lifetime, you have developed a value for experiencing other cultures and seeing historical sights. Driven by that value, you work to create travel experiences for your family and exchange programs for your students.

3. **Negative orientation to past memories:** Here, you are attached to some form of memory that did not meet your expectation, and you are driven either to right the wrong or to compensate for the resulting shortcoming.
   - *Example*—As a child, you never had an opportunity to travel, due to reasons beyond your control. As a result, you are motivated to create travel opportunities both for your family and for your students.

4. **Negative orientation to future expectations:** A negative future orientation is characterized by a perception of an impending threat. You look ahead with fear and are motivated to prevent the manifestation of that threat, or at least the outcome of it.

⌑ *Example*—You experience trepidation about the disadvantage that your family or students may face if they do not experience travel as they grow up. To avoid this, you feel driven to provide them with experiences to overcome this deficit.

In each of these situations, you are motivated to take some form of action based on the application of a value or ideal. The previous examples highlight similar outcomes based in similar values, yet the source of motivation for each is subtly different. If you consider each of these scenarios as if they were different people, each would bring a different experience to the decision to travel. By understanding the basis of how you make decisions, you can consider a fuller range of factors influencing your thoughts.

Recovering From a Loss of Volition

This choice is at the very center of the importance of volition as a core component of motivation. Volition is the power of choice. There are reasons why you do everything that you do—even when those reasons live far beneath your awareness. Those components of volition that live above the line of your awareness are readily accessible, both as a source of affirmation when things go well and as a source of support when they do not. You know why you do what you do, and you are aware of the outcomes produced by your efforts. This awareness propels you to press on. So, what happens when you either lose touch with your volition or, at the very least, lose your awareness of it? Questions regarding the substance of your work begin to go unanswered. You become unmotivated. You begin to experience disillusionment or even burnout. Or at least you think you are.

There are very few people in this world who truly have nothing at all to motivate them. Instead, many people either are unaware of what motivates them or are in roles not connected to that source of motivation. The short circuit in the process of volitional awareness comes from three primary areas.

1. You lose awareness of why you are working toward a goal.
2. Your source of motivation changes because of a significant life event.
3. You apply a judgment of that source of motivation that devalues it.

Loss of awareness is perhaps the most common. In the full nature of a school leader's days, your time is thoroughly occupied by the matter of the moment. You have promises to keep and many people to whom you have made them. That is the nature of your work. If there are to be moments committed to authentic reflection within your day, they would most certainly be brief and scheduled intentionally. They don't just happen. You have scheduling issues, student management challenges, staff concerns, building matters, and a variety of other challenges that vie for your attention every day. It is the nature of your work. Your job is to create and preserve the environment in which your teachers teach and your learners learn. That means you will always be chasing something. The smoother things appear to the outside eye, the harder you are working to maintain that perception. In the busyness and the clamor of those days, it is small wonder that you become fixated on the minutia, often sacrificing what forms your deeper sense of purpose. Where is there room for *why*?

Adapting to Changes in Volition

If you haven't lost sight of your sense of purpose, what happens when the basis for that sense of purpose changes altogether? Life will at times conspire to challenge you in new and unanticipated ways—the outcome of such challenges can impact what is most important to you. But, if the concepts and values that guide your decision making are so foundational, why would they change at all? Shouldn't they remain consistent throughout your career? That might be a valid assertion if *you* remained the same over the course of your career. Clearly, you do not. Your experiences inform your beliefs as you grow and develop both personally and professionally. You evolve as a person—so it stands to reason that the course of your volition would change as well. Life situations also change. You may be motivated by the need to support your children through college, but what happens when they graduate? You may be driven by the need to see your school through a difficult crisis, but what happens when that crisis passes? People often fail to recognize the importance of maintaining flexibility in what forms the foundation of their beliefs. People evolve.

Finally, you come to the challenge of applying a value judgment to the source of your volition. Nowhere is this more evident, nor more damaging, than in the world of education. You are expected to center your work on the more intrinsic values of fulfillment and the betterment of society. In some ways, feeling good about what you do is part of your compensation. You work to improve your students' lives and the world they will enter. None of this is bad, and all of it is valid. That said, in applying such values across circumstances, there is a danger of minimizing possible extrinsic rewards. Is there room in the volitional profile for the value of earning money to support one's family? Can we be competent and constructive educators who see vacations and summer as part of the reward?

The most important element of volition and maintaining it over time is the connection it brings to your values. These values are part of who you are as a person and are fundamental parts of what motivates you. Each person is accountable for their decisions and the foundation they're based on. You are also the benefactor of the motivation that they bring.

Applied to leadership, an awareness of the underlying values and how they are oriented to the decision at hand allows you to remain connected to the ultimate source of your motivation. You are aware of why you do this work and continue to be driven by it as you choose to accept the challenges of leadership each day. This drive forms a core component of leadership capacity. By remaining connected to the source of your volition, you can work at the upper limits of your capabilities in a given moment.

Looking at Spirituality as an Element of Volition

School leaders, particularly those public school educators who live in the world of nonsecular purposes, are often reluctant to delve into matters of faith, spirituality, or religion. In addition to the constitutional separation of church and state in the United States, matters of faith are also deeply personal and potentially sensitive to many. Even in making this statement, I recognize the different comfort levels will lead people in different directions. The matter of spiritual belief and faith forms an important motivation for many people, and to leave it unacknowledged in this book would render any consideration of motivation incomplete. Regardless of what you believe about the larger structure of life, the way humanity was created, and why you are here, the founding elements of your personal worldview form a base on which you build your sense of purpose. Faith, religion, traditions, and worldviews all contribute to your sense of purpose and, with it, the reasons you do what you do.

In a fundamental sense, faith and religion are an embodiment of the ways in which people consider questions that have unknowable answers. In the broader sense, the Editors of Encyclopaedia Britannica (2024) define *religion* as follows:

> Religion, human beings' relation to that which they regard as holy, sacred, absolute, spiritual, divine, or worthy of especial reverence. It is also commonly regarded as consisting of the way people deal with ultimate concerns about their lives and their fate after death.

Religious beliefs articulate values that guide people's lives. Those values, in turn, can guide the decisions that you make as you move through your days. They form, by definition, the substance of your volition.

In the context of examining motivation, focus on the matter of people's beliefs about their own fate or purpose. Many religions espouse a life of service to others as a foundation either for a fulfilling life or as part of a moral code to which believers must adhere to gain a reward in an afterlife. Both beliefs support an intrinsic basis for motivation and, more specifically, for the service elements of educating young people.

Naturally, faith and religion hold significance well beyond volition. Many religions promote varying approaches to meditation or prayer that form an approach to de-escalation and reflection. One example is found in Buddhist practices, where "meditation techniques have arisen from the Buddha's insights about the nature of existence, the causes of suffering, the causes of happiness, and guidelines for living a wholesome and constructive life" (Mendel, n.d.). Some advanced teachings that deal specifically with conduct address what should or should not be done in matters of physical health. In Judaism, the laws of Kashrut articulate what foods can or cannot be eaten and how they are to be prepared as directed by the Torah (Jewish Virtual Library, n.d.). Still other elements of religions provide practitioners with significant sources of support through emotional trials, giving a sense of belonging that may be missing in the daily practice of leadership. This sense of community and belonging is particularly important in Christianity, where the practice of *fellowship* comes from the Greek word *koinonia*, which refers to "holding something in common" (Cardoza, 2021). Beliefs and faith are a deeply personal matter in all aspects of life—they impact the substance of how people make decisions. All are significant resources that can sustain leaders as they seek balance and a sense of purpose that are crucial parts of leading at the outer limits of your capacity.

This address of religion and faith is not in any way intended to promote the practice of one religion over another anymore than it is intended to advocate spirituality as a mandatory element of support. It is, instead, intended to acknowledge the significant source of support and motivation that a faith tradition supplies to those who choose to practice them, in whatever form that comes. As you seek out elements of your life that motivate you, there are significant merits to a full consideration of that which supports and sustains you. Anything less would leave a full range of variables unacknowledged that are available to support optimal performance levels.

Seeing Why Authentic Reflection Is Crucial to Leadership

Not all your decisions are made in direct connection to values or volition. The fast pace and demanding nature of your work require you to react quickly and in pragmatic ways. At times this requires you to do things that you might later regret. How, then, do you come to understand those decisions and move beyond them? Once again, the key lies in a level of self-awareness that leads to authentic reflection.

The human brain is capable of tremendous feats of rationalization. You look at the context of a situation through your biases and values. Sometimes, that process works to your advantage by guiding you toward a decision consistent with this internal compass. Other times, you can talk yourself into what can become a less positive decision, like topping off a delicious meal with a big slice of pie. What's the difference? It all comes from your awareness and your purpose.

People often avoid the truth of a situation in their own momentary interest. Far from just a matter of rationalizing a piece of pie, people also look to justify to themselves and others the decisions they have made or are about to make. They focus on the elements of that decision that are the least disruptive to their peace of mind in a moment. For the purposes of this topic, avoid the temptation to look down some kind of ethical rabbit hole of justification. Instead, look at the ways in which you justify decisions that seem pertinent in a moment but have long-reaching impacts on your capacity to carry out leadership responsibilities. You enter the demands of a given circumstance, bracketing it with both your conscious thought and subconscious contextual compass.

For example, consider how events might unfold if a principal were confronted with an emotionally charged disciplinary matter in the middle of a fire drill. Alarms are blaring, the stopwatch is ticking, and amid it all, this leader must now confront unsafe or illegal behavior. The leader is called on to manage multiple facets of emotional behavior. It's little wonder if the person should choose a functional approach to both situations rather than take a more deliberate tact that might normally be called for. The moment must be managed—sensitivity and deliberation will come later. In this example, the principal must make a judgment call as to whether the severity of the disciplinary matter warrants ignoring the fire alarm or if the issue can be addressed after the alarm. The decision is made in the heat of the moment based on safety and without the opportunity to decide on the values expressed. Regardless of the principal's choice, the situation must be evaluated within the pace and emotion of the moment.

Every day, you do what you must to press through such moments safely. You do your best to manage the circumstances in a way that reflects the kind of fairness and composure that is a core element of your values. That said, exceptions can occur when you are either hurried or taxed by multiple competing situations. In your reactions, you are infinitely human.

You may wish that you had handled such instances differently, and of course, there are people both within your schools and in your communities who were watching. The key element of such moments, regardless of what actions you take within them, is to be able to step away and recognize the effects of your choices. You need not justify them or defend them—if you do something that wasn't in line with your values, you can still seek to understand it, acknowledge it, and rectify it. Your presumptions, most likely, are based on the idea that you always make the best decisions that you can based on who you are in that moment. Reflection and adjustments follow given the benefit of time and space. Such steps are a way for you to remain consistent with your core sense of values and motivation while understanding the impact of a given situation on your decision-making process.

But your days are so full. Who has time for weekly retreats or extended meditation sessions? Classifying authentic reflection as an act specific to one format or another prevents you from engaging in it on a regular basis. Yes, for some, formal meditation practice is an outstanding way to recharge and think deeply about your practice. That's certainly not true of everyone, though. The key conditions needed for reflection are an opportunity to remove oneself from the operational environment and a safe, quiet environment in which to engage in deeper contextual thoughts about the question at hand. By that definition, you can engage in real and substantive reflection in a far greater range of contexts in accordance with your lifestyle and interests.

A few activities or environments that can be conducive to reflective thinking include the following.

- **Cardiovascular exercise:** Cycling, walking, rowing, and running
- **Outdoor activities or hobbies:** Hiking, fishing, geocaching, and gardening
- **Creative outlets:** Painting, drawing, photography, and crafts
- **Chores or tasks:** Mowing the lawn, cleaning the house, laundry, and home repair projects

In each of these cases, you are removed from the work environment and engaged in activities that still allow you to think on matters that confront you. As a bonus, these activities also benefit physical wellness and cognitive de-escalation. They are multipurpose, which makes them easier to schedule and engage in. The key element to any of these reflective environments is that they are meaningful to you, and they result in an opportunity for genuine reflection.

By contextualizing your reflective practice within your personal interests, you create space to think deeply about your work in an environment and a time that is sustainable. You prioritize that element of your capacity in a way that is both real and easier for you to prioritize. Many of these things are already a part of your daily life and need only to be recontextualized as reflection opportunities.

Surrounding Yourself With Your Why

This chapter has looked at the ways a solid grounding in a sense of purpose can sustain you through the inherent challenges of leading schools. By maintaining connection with the source of your motivation, you can lessen the long-term impact of burnout or disillusionment that can progress as you wear down. By building from authentic reflection and an awareness of your volition, you can take a more active approach to staying connected to the reasons you do what you do—even when they seem out of reach at times.

Your efforts should begin by acknowledging what you are working through. Take a moment to acknowledge your current state. Interoception is usually a subconscious process, and you generally adapt without realizing it. By taking a moment to monitor the full spectrum of your physical body and cognitive processing, you are better able to recognize how these states are affecting your frame of mind. You can see what your current state is doing to your thought processes. You can see why you are feeling as you are and can take steps to overcome it.

What does this look like in practice? Examine the following ideas for how school leaders can create space in their day to stay motivated.

1. **Connecting with students:** Nearly all educators enter the profession motivated by the desire for fulfillment and the sense of satisfaction that comes from working with students. One of the realities of taking on a leadership role is that leaders are separated from that immediate, regular connection, at least for the most part. They can stay in touch

with that element of their work by actively seeking opportunities to connect with students in a positive way.

2. **Connecting with a love of a particular topic or content:** Many educators found their entry point into the profession through a connection with some specific element of their own learning. Whether through academic content, cocurricular activities, or athletics, you can find opportunities to reconnect as well. There are as many ways to do so as there are things to do. You need only look.

3. **Connecting with family or friends:** This is the meeting point of social needs and motivation. Education is a highly interpersonal profession, but it is not a social environment. You may be motivated by a need to provide for your family—and you should remind yourself of that by spending time with them. You may also be motivated by the camaraderie that is part of the educational profession. It serves you well to spend time with like-minded peers. In either case, you are connecting with your sense of purpose.

4. **Connecting with the outdoors:** As mentioned in chapter 4 (page 73), there is reliable information supporting the benefits of spending time outdoors, no matter where you live and work. Whether for physical, cognitive, or emotional well-being, time spent in the fresh air is never wasted. For health benefits, opportunities for reflection become compelling pieces of the puzzle of your volition.

5. **Connecting with a cause:** Educators find value in ideas. It is an integral part of what they do. They teach their students to acquire information, process it, evaluate it, create it, and even dispute it. The generation and transmission of ideas are the foundation of everything they do. So, what then of their own ideas? Often leaders become so preoccupied with their work to facilitate learning that they forget their own love of and connection with ideas. Finding ideas with which to engage and connecting with a cause are healthy parts of sustaining yourself in the work. Whether through book clubs, social organizations, or peer groups, you can sustain your energy—and with it your capacity—by remembering those causes that are valuable to you.

Education is a selfless profession. While you come to work motivated by your own set of variables, you are a caretaker. You work to support your learners. You lead in education because you care deeply about the manner and direction of the larger system and believe that you can impact it in a positive manner. While you recognize your own roles and interests within the day, it is not in a leader's nature to think of themselves first. You construct mindsets that ignore, if not devalue, your own sense of well-being, and you do not recognize that, in doing so, you prevent yourself from working at the outer limits of your potential, skills, and abilities.

By widening the scope of professional development to include all the variables that impact performance, you endorse the value of capacity in the work. Like so many elite athletes, leaders see the long-term benefit of this broader scope in the work they do with learners. They take care of themselves so that each morning they arrive at school as prepared as possible to be their best selves. The work will not get easier any time soon. It is up to you to think differently about how best to prepare for it. The next chapter will tie everything together so you can put it all into practice.

Questions for Reflection

Use the following questions to help you reflect on what you have read in this chapter.

1. Why did you decide to pursue a career in education?
2. What factors influenced your decision to pursue a leadership position? Have your experiences thus far supported these factors?
3. What are your three most rewarding experiences, both as a school leader and within the profession as a whole?
4. Where do you turn for support when you feel frustrated or unmotivated at work? What resources do you have to push through those challenging days?
5. Are there any circumstances where you would consider leaving the profession prior to retirement? If so, what resources might you put in place to support you should those circumstances ever occur?

Uncovering Your Volition

This book has referred to the root cause of why you choose to be a leader in an educational environment as your volition—the act of making a choice. One common element in any attempt to clarify your volition or motivation is the importance of stories. These stories form the raw materials on which you build your understanding of your volition in the present day. This activity prompts you to recall the stories that have shaped your entry both into the educational profession and into the realm of leadership.

1. What was your first position in the education field? What brought you to accept this position?

2. What were the most rewarding parts of this job?

3. In what ways have you experienced these rewarding experiences in subsequent jobs of a similar type?

4. What were your three fondest memories of this work?

5. What reasons would you give to others who are contemplating this work to enter this position?

6. What is the earliest memory you have of contemplating the transition into a leadership position? What made you think that this transition would be a good fit for you?

7. What was your first leadership position? Why did you choose to apply and accept the position?

8. What have been your three fondest memories from your time as a school leader?

9. What part of your current role do you look forward to most?

10. What would you like to add into your schedule, whether it's something you aren't able to do anymore or something you love to do that you don't do enough?

11. What is the most fulfilling part of your current role?

12. If you were to speak to a group of aspiring school leaders, what would you tell them are the three best reasons to become one?

Analyzing Your Responses

To help you find those stories that are most crucial to your source of motivation, consider each in the following contexts.

- If you were to share one story with a group of aspiring teachers, which would you choose?

- If you were to select one story at a ceremony in your honor, which would you choose?

- If you were to write an article featuring one of these stories, which would you choose?

- If you were to tell a story at a family gathering, which would you choose?

Now, look at your responses in each of these contexts. What do they have in common? What values do you see in each of them? Do any of these values recur? The recurring or consistent themes of these stories reveal the source of your motivation—the insight into your volition.

By maintaining regular opportunities to reflect in a manner that is authentic for you, you allow yourself to remain connected to the source of your motivation. Each day, you make a choice to reengage as a school leader. Knowing why you make that choice is a key element to avoiding feelings of disillusionment, disconnection, and a lack of fulfillment.

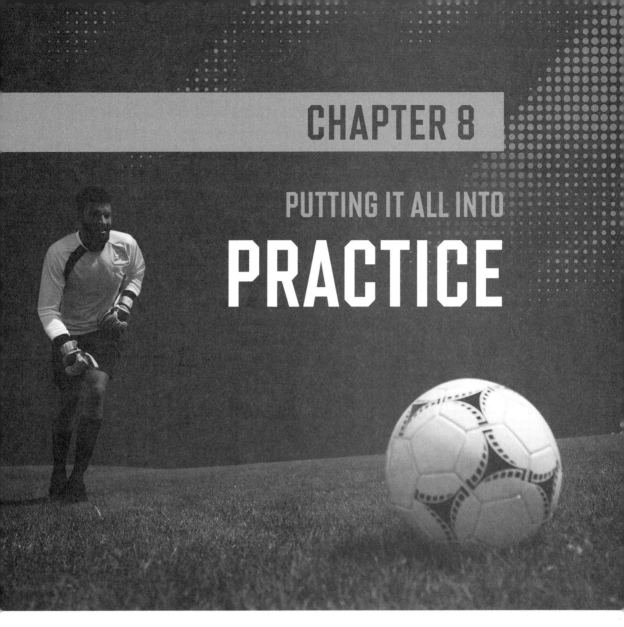

CHAPTER 8

PUTTING IT ALL INTO PRACTICE

Athletes Have a Plan

In competitive sports, everyone has a plan. Tactics and strategy are key elements in preparing for competition and often determine the outcome. The degree to which that plan works depends largely on two factors: (1) whether it is a good plan and (2) whether it is implemented well. The quality of the plan is relative to the circumstances, available resources, and extraneous variables. You have a lot more control over the implementation of the plan. Implementation is a process that comes from an awareness of the existing environment, the required resources, and, most of all, the people charged with making it all happen.

For example, take the implementation of a tactical game plan in soccer. As a very strategic sport, the outcomes of games are often determined by tactical decisions and advanced preparation. Once a coach has developed a plan for the upcoming match, they must teach it to the team in a way team members understand and can execute given their respective skill levels. They practice the plan leading up to the match, including potential adjustments for changes occurring as the game unfolds. They learn to respond within the natural flow of a game, and they anticipate the possible outlier experiences that could occur. As the game begins, the team is as prepared as possible to implement their plan to be successful. Then, much of the response is up to the players.

Not unlike leading a school, coaching a sports team is an experience that features a moment of powerlessness. Once the competition begins, a coach has limited ability to impact the flow of the game. Yes, the team relies on the coach to make adjustments and substitutions, but the competitors themselves determine the outcome. This process illustrates the importance of a sound approach to implementing a plan, including adaptations under foreseeable complications. This mindset is no different in a school. When you think of the strategies that you employ to develop your leadership capacity on an ongoing basis, there are plans or strategies already in place at some points, and others where you are left to your own efforts. You execute a plan to the greatest degree possible, knowing that the flow of the game will require you to adapt.

Once you know what you need to remain healthy and strong to work at the outer limits of your capacity, the process of putting those conditions in place becomes compulsory. You owe it to the students in your charge, to the faculty and staff you lead, to the communities you serve, and—most of all—to your family and yourself. It is not selfish to prioritize well-being; it is a mandatory element of being the best leader you can be. Therefore, if you are to function at the outer limits of your capacity within an inherently complex environment, you need to expand your understanding of the variables affecting your performance.

The purpose of this book, as previously stated, is to raise school leaders' awareness of the impact of physical, cognitive, emotional, and motivational factors on the quality and sustainability of their work. These areas are seldom covered by traditional professional development programs, yet their impact is clear. Nearly all school systems have some form of professional learning approach for their leaders—and the surest way for the priorities outlined in this book to fail would be to simply add them on top of what is already expected of school leaders. Leaders barely have the time and headspace to follow through with the expectations currently in place. Adding more to it will actively work against their efforts to increase capacity. Therefore, how can you introduce more elements to professional development without adding more time? You need to make better choices by using competencies as a practical approach in a busy schedule, knowing how to assess your strengths and weaknesses, using sources of data to track your growth, finding support, and creating your own personal approach.

The reproducible, "Building Motivational Clarity Into Your Existing Evaluation Process" (page 159), is intended to bridge the discussion of motivation from chapter 7 (page 125) with the integration of these concepts into your current approach to managing professional learning. These questions focus on practical opportunities to emphasize capacity within the structure of what you already do.

Using Competencies as a Practical Approach in a Busy Schedule

In chapter 2 (page 29), you looked at the ways in which current thinking regarding competency-based learning for students might be helpful in planning your own development. Tenets such as learning based on mastery rather than time, targeted interventions, and a personalized approach to content being studied all apply easily here. For example, for a school leader who runs marathons as a hobby, cardiovascular fitness would not be her biggest priority. That leader has demonstrated ongoing competency. Instead, that leader may need to work with mental rehearsal, motivational clarity, or some other element impacting performance. Therefore, you begin your assessment of capacity with an inventory of your most pressing current needs, juxtaposed with the elements of leadership that you already demonstrate. What emerges is a clear image of where best to spend your valuable time and resources relative to expanding your capacity.

The following are three keys to implementing a competency-based approach to capacity building that is authentic and sustainable.

1. **Planning and delivery of these plans should be part of the existing approach to professional learning:** Activities should be considered part of that work, not added in as an expectation on top of it. If they are valued and clearly identified as needs, the activities developed within your plans may *replace* existing professional development work.

2. **The approach should be implemented across a system, building, or district:** It can't be framed as "something Janet or Bob is doing" within the professional community. However, it can be framed as something that your leadership team is doing. An important element for sustainability is for the broader community to understand capacity development and to see their leaders' actions as key elements of it. This isn't a fad or an afterthought. It is a refocusing of priorities.

3. **Plans should be developed by individual leaders in accordance with their individual needs and demonstrated competencies:** In larger districts, there may be opportunities to group leaders with common needs or goals, but the measurement of these goals is individual. This is an ideal place to develop a connection to existing sources of support from both an evaluative and developmental capacity. One of the most feasible elements of this approach is the concentration of time and resources on leaders' individual needs. Less time and money are wasted on unnecessary professional development.

The format of the individual planning process is flexible enough to incorporate into a variety of professional development and evaluation systems. Regardless of the approach or system used in a school district, nearly all districts can accommodate personalized projects, action research, or targeted performance interventions. This approach entails working at a broader scope to identify any specific variables that impact performance—even if they are not incorporated into conventional standards or expectations. What is most important is adhering to an expanded definition of capacity development. Leaders will be better at the work they do if they pay attention to a broader understanding of performance.

This approach to professional learning need not supplant existing systems in place for record keeping, standards, expectations, or formats. This is particularly true for schools or districts that have professional development systems in place that are a part of a collective bargaining agreement. (Clearly, any different approach or strategy needs to be discussed with the appropriate associations, just as in any other case where changes are contemplated.) The concept of competency-based professional learning for leaders may be implemented at the procedural level.

A few examples of this idea might include the following.

- Set goals as part of a formalized reflection and self-evaluation process. Most leadership development models include some form of goal-setting model, often indexed from district goals or expectations. While such an approach is highly beneficial in creating common outcomes across a district, the addition of personalized goal setting indexed to capacity development will afford leaders the opportunity they need to engage in relevant, high-impact activities.

- Structure professional learning days, workshops, or retreats around differentiated learning opportunities—participation could be responsive to leaders with identified needs or learning requirements. Leaders might also have the opportunity to opt out of a professional development experience if they had already demonstrated that learning.

- Facilitate embedded assessment by developing a means of recording pertinent professional experiences that leaders encounter within the context of their work. Leaders are expected to adhere to standards of performance within the work they do—why not develop a means of documenting what they do every day that demonstrates these standards? A format doesn't need to be complex or outside of an existing system. Leaders only need the opportunity to recognize how the work they do demonstrates levels of competency in expected areas.

Naturally, these suggestions are intended only to provide interested districts with a starting point for implementing a system that supports the advancement of leadership capacity. They are not a blanket solution but a starting point. As the understanding of and value for leadership capacity takes root within a district, greater time and effort can be placed on how to facilitate this work. The potential is staggering.

Although a succinct and personalized experience for advancing leadership capacity is the goal, there is, of course, an opportunity to engage in this process in a much deeper way. Figure 1.2 (page 21 in chapter 1) showed a potential organizational model that provided a framework for a more substantive integration of the leadership capacity concept.

This broader approach to capacity building and professional growth is intended to provide a starting point for districts that may aspire to develop a specific and more detailed approach. It incorporates the placement of existing standards and competencies in the external position while establishing a context for the internal competencies that form the subject of this book. While far from a plug-in program, this framework can allow for schools or districts to engage in a more substantive effort to build a capacity-based approach that is tailored to the specific needs and resources of the community.

Assessing Your Own Strengths and Weaknesses

As is the case with any learning, the most important part of getting started is to understand where the learner is at the outset. Educators do this with students. By understanding what students know and can do, teachers can focus on what areas require focus to achieve desired learning outcomes. This approach is no different for you as you consider your own development. By structuring a deliberate approach to understanding the limitations of your current performance level, you focus on what to work on first and what may be less in need of your attention. Here, the domains that have been established in the preceding chapters provide a starting point to reflect on the elements of performance that you have already connected to leadership capacity.

- **Physical and physiological capacity:** How do you feel? Are there elements of your physical health that in any way limit your ability to perform leadership tasks at optimal levels? Many leaders have been taught to push through illness or pain, remaining on the job when health may be impeding their performance. Are you currently doing this, even if detrimental to your performance level?
    - *Frequency of illness, even if it does not result in absence from work*—Do you notice that physical ailments either detract from your ability to attend to work or result in frequent needs to call in sick?
    - *Chronic pain or health impairments, inflammation, or other health concerns*—Are you currently managing any chronic or recurring health conditions that distract from your ability to attend to work? If so, are you following the advice of your health care provider?
    - *Ongoing energy deficit beyond expected levels of fatigue*— Here we make the distinction between acute fatigue and the more chronic variety. This goes well beyond just being tired. How often do you find yourself drowsy or unable to focus during a meeting or presentation?
    - *Elements of allostatic load impacting well-being or optimal performance*—In what ways does the cumulative impact of stress activation show up in the way you feel physically each day?

- **Cognitive and mental capacity:** Do you wake up each morning with a clear head and a feeling of being well rested? Do you experience mental clarity on a regular basis? Do you struggle to focus? Does fatigue or distraction impact your daily work?
    - *Healthy sleep habits, both in time slept and quality of sleep*—Do you get at least six hours of quality sleep each day?
    - *Parasympathetic de-escalation, returning to calm after a crisis*—Are you able to return to a calm and composed state in short order following a challenging situation? Do you use any specific strategies, or are you able to do so naturally?
    - *Imposing an artificial circadian rhythm using sleep aids, chemical substances, or other forms of stimulants or depressants*—Are you able to sleep and wake at regular times without supplements?
    - *Prolonged or frequent stress activation, possibly during times or events that are not seemingly stressful in nature*—Are you exhibiting signs of stress during times that are not inherently stressful?
    - *Sympathetic response to stressors*—Are you recognizing cognitive activation of your sympathetic response, through either remembering past stressors or anticipating potential upcoming events?
- **Emotional capacity:** Are you able to regulate your emotions to a degree where you have a positive impact on your school environment? Do you maintain appropriate emotional outlets to maintain your own well-being? Do you experience emotional challenges outside of work that complicate your time within work?
    - *Available support*—Are you aware of supports that are available to you through either your employer or another community-sponsored resource? Sources of emotional support are available, both within the constraints of your professional work and in your personal life, as needed.
    - *Social needs impact performance levels*—Are your social needs being met? How might that happen? Optimal levels of performance emerge from maintaining emotional balance, and one element of that balance is engaged in all pertinent emotional needs being met.

¤ *Mental rehearsal and stress reactions*—Are you using anticipation and planning as a means of lessening a psychological stress response. Are you able to facilitate emotional preparedness for upcoming and potential events at the appropriate times and places? Do you plan for or simulate situations that may be emotionally charged or unusually stressful?

¤ *Resources for support*—Are you aware of potential resources at your disposal to which you can turn if you need more comprehensive support?

- **Motivational capacity:** Do you have a clear picture of what motivates you? Have you had the opportunity to reflect deeply on it? What is your why?

    ¤ *Structured opportunities for regular reflection, specifically within circumstances and settings that allow the individual person to do so in an authentic manner*—How do you best move beyond pro forma reflection?

    ¤ *Environmental reminders of your source of motivation*—You are better able to maintain a connection to your volition and resulting decisions if you build in some form of reminder of their substance. Again, authenticity is key here. What can you put in place that will serve as a permanent reminder of what motivates you?

    ¤ *Collective or systemwide acknowledgment of institutional goals and the recognition of individual volition*—Schools tend to be adept at incorporating institutional goals or visions into their environment, but how can you best recognize and value the goals of the individuals who make up these schools? This extends well beyond the development of individual goals through a professional development program.

    ¤ *Support for volition*—Are you aware of groups, activities, or communities that are supportive of your personal source of volition? This could include anything from professional associations, faith communities, or social causes to which you feel committed. By surrounding yourself with people who are committed to the same values, you affirm their impact and remain connected to them.

By engaging in a broader examination of these components, leaders can gain insights into the elements that may be limiting their capacity as a starting point for the planning process. Again, the ways in which plans are developed and written should be consistent with the existing professional development and assessment systems of your district.

Using Sources of Data to Track Your Growth

Once areas of focus have been identified for each individual leader and goals have been articulated within the structure of their professional development process, the next step is to identify the most efficient means of measuring performance levels. As is the case with all these factors, there is no passing grade; the drive to improve comes from within each leader. Instead, data should be collected in a way that recognizes authentic progress. Measurement is intended to facilitate growth—not acceptance. In this way, standards and expectations can be personalized, focused, and ordered. Capacity, in this context, becomes a designation of the upper limits of individual performance. It denotes what each school leader can do under optimal conditions and within the structure of both their role and circumstances.

If you are starting a cardiovascular fitness plan for the first time, your doctor may be able to help you identify a means of measuring progress. It could be time walked, distance over time, heart rate elevation, or another preset variable or measure of achievement. This is a contest only with yourself. The goal is yours and so is the progress. The supervisory component is built around your progress, not your achievement. (Can you imagine a superintendent requiring members of their administrative team to run a mile in a prescribed time? Definitely *not* the point here.) The domain itself expresses a value for cardiovascular well-being to prepare the body for the demands of this work—for frequent or prolonged activation of your stress response. Where each person begins, how far they travel, and how they get there within the realm of heart health is something far more personal.

In much the same way, the establishment of means of measuring cognitive, emotional, and motivational well-being are also intended to track growth. It would be counterproductive to introduce elements of external competitiveness into any of these areas, but developing means of measuring each gives you tangible goals or expectations.

Other potential means of measuring growth in or commitment to these elements include the following.

- Cognitive well-being
    - You can measure sleep quantity and quality through a sleep tracker, either on a fitness tracker device or on a dedicated sleep monitor. If a less technical approach is more appealing, you can keep a sleep journal measuring times and quality. By measuring sleep on an ongoing basis, you can juxtapose the different elements of your lifestyle that impact sleep quality, resulting in opportunities to make adjustments that bring positive impacts.
    - You can quantify and schedule both daily opportunities for de-escalation and reflection, either at predetermined parts of your day or at surrounding events that you know to be common stressors. Once again, by scheduling or recording these windows of time, you can monitor the regularity with which you commit to them, as well as understanding the degrees of outcome from them.
- Emotional well-being
    - Measuring your emotional well-being is a matter of creating opportunities for genuine reflection. You cannot benefit from the type of self-awareness needed to remain emotionally aware without it. Therefore, measuring emotional well-being is more a matter of measuring time and opportunity committed to reflecting on it. You bring the most important settings and methods of reflection, and you create a predetermined amount of time to it on a regular basis. You measure the frequency and duration of opportunity, and you commit to it.
    - The practice of mental rehearsal allows leaders to develop broader conceptual preparation for emotionally charged situations and manage the fallout of these unavoidable elements of their work. By incorporating regularly scheduled, comprehensive sessions involving this practice, leaders can both prepare themselves for how they regulate their emotions during these moments, as well as reduce the anxiety before them in anticipation and after them in review. As is the case with other elements, this is only beneficial if you schedule sessions regularly and commit to them. Measurement comes from this degree of commitment and produces tangible results.

- Other methods of measuring emotional well-being in relation to capacity are hinged largely on time and access to resources. If your emotional well-being requires access to a formal counseling program, you commit to it and schedule it as a part of your day. If this requires forgoing other scheduled events, you justify the decision to do so by the wider commitment to maximized capacity. You cannot work at the outer limits of your ability if you aren't adhering to the requirements you experience relative to emotional well-being.

- Motivational clarity
  - Measuring motivational clarity is a much more difficult task, though not impossible. By codifying a daily motivational check-in, you can track your level of energy, commitment, or positive outlook, resulting in a traceable pattern over time and circumstance. This check-in can be incorporated into daily calendars, journals, or other resources you consult daily.
  - You can also quantify regular access to those elements of your life that form the core of your volition. If you are working for your family, scheduling regular family time is a must. If you are driven by working with students, you can quantify such things as classroom visits, recess, or lunchtime exposure to students or structured opportunities for after-school work with student groups.

Finding Opportunities for Support

A variety of potential sources of support exist in all domains within the professional community of leaders. An important element of leadership capacity is developing a familiarity with what is already available to you through district programs, professional associations, and health insurance providers, or to the broader community of practice in which you work.

In establishing a new and broader definition of what it means to develop your work as a leader, it's important to acknowledge the importance of connecting to resources that you have at your disposal that you do not currently use. Naturally, this varies by district or state. This makes it even more important that you actively pursue awareness of these resources within the structure of your capacity-building efforts.

If you don't know what you have, you will not be able to benefit from the full range of resources even in advance of creating new ones. Just as you look to integrate your efforts into your current model of professional learning, you recognize the importance of not duplicating or replacing support elements already at your disposal.

Even when a specific resource may not currently be available in your district, it is well worth the time to inquire whether an opportunity could be created. For example, take a specific fitness activity. Where an individual might be drawn to cycling as a form of cardiovascular exercise, a district may not offer a cycling club (for staff or students), but there may be sufficient interest to develop one through an employee-wellness program or intramural league. It never hurts to explore such possibilities within your district. The closer an activity remains to your work, the more readily it can be accessed and sustained over time.

The following is a closer look at some of the practices that may not be a regular part of a school leader's day but could benefit your leadership capacity.

- **Yearly wellness evaluation:** Leadership teams, districts, or schools can establish a common set of wellness goal areas—such as those that form the structure of this book—and include them in an annual process where individual leaders examine their state of well-being relative to those different elements. This process can be included in a retreat, year-end goal setting, or a variety of other events.

- **Authentic reflection:** Examine the required reflections included in existing district processes. The purpose is to make any outcomes more authentic. Does your district take the matter of reflection seriously, or is it relatively pro forma? What are your anticipated outcomes? How are those outcomes used to monitor levels of progress toward proficiency or valid learning?

- **Facilitated mental rehearsal:** Mental rehearsal can be used to decrease the impact of a psychologically induced stress activation. By preparing leaders to deal effectively with potentially stressful situations, they are less likely to experience the impacts of anticipated stress on allostatic load. This preparation requires a school or district to commit to the process of regularly scheduled facilitated rehearsals centered on situations that are stress inducing.

- **Motivational clarity:** Leaders commit to regular reflection as a means of remaining connected to their source of motivation. This commitment is built in conjunction with school or district goal setting, not instead of it. By maintaining awareness of your volition, you strengthen your commitment to your profession and support your efforts to overcome potential burnout and depletion.

- **Catalog of learning resources:** All districts and schools have professional learning resources at their disposal, and yet few take the time to communicate those resources relative to professional expectations. While this requires an initial investment of time to set it up and organize these resources, this catalog can be used to structure competency-based learning experiences of varying sorts. It is also an effective way to learn what a district has, and what it needs to expand on.

Creating Your Personal Approach to Meaningful Reflection

There are many different environments that are conducive to authentic reflection, ranging from formal meditative environments to creating personal space within your schedule. As previously discussed, building in time for this element is a way to advance your cognitive functioning, emotional well-being, and an ongoing awareness of your sources of motivation.

This benefit does not necessarily require you to implement a formal meditation practice. If you look at the meditative process as an active attempt to de-escalate and clarify your thoughts, there are many ways to go about this. Just as is the case with exercise, it is far more likely that you will commit to reflection on an ongoing basis if you find ways to engage in it that are consistent with your interests and priorities. This approach means taking a broader definition of reflection that removes the mind from the regular analytical, task-focused processes that you are committed to while leading schools.

So, what can reflective time look like if you take this broader approach? The wider environment would involve removing yourself from your physical work setting and from the commitment of attention for a predetermined period. The demands of your day distract you from inward-facing thought in favor of more functional thinking. Only by removing yourself from that functional environment can you truly reflect. This need not be for hours or days—instead, just a short, committed period during which you intentionally focus inward on your thoughts, state of mind, and an awareness of the details of your physical functioning. The following are a few of the different environments that are conducive to such reflection.

- Quiet time during exercise
- Formal meditation, prayer, or contemplation
- Time spent in a setting that you find peaceful, such as a walk in a favorite park
- Participation in a hobby or interest that allows for mental refocus, such as fishing, hiking, a bicycle ride, or other activities that allow for a quiet mind
- Distraction in more active ways, such as listening to music or reading

While formal meditation practice has tremendous value, there are a variety of different ways by which you can clear your mind and engage in authentic reflection. These approaches are personal, and the most important outcome is for you to identify the most effective and sustainable approach for you.

With this established, it is also important to acknowledge the viability of a more traditional approach to meditation practice. For those interested in exploring the benefits of meditation but lacking any formal training or experience in it, an excellent starting point is *Stress Less, Accomplish More: Meditation for Extraordinary Performance* by Emily Fletcher (2019), which provides an overview of the benefits meditation offers in a way that focuses on the mental and physical elements of practice and is an accessible approach for beginners. It also leads to other resources that can provide deeper learning for those interested in more than an introduction.

Ultimately, each person must find an approach to reflection that is authentic and meaningful in their own lives. This allows you to slow down the pace of your work, to think through your experiences, and to find meaning in the daily challenges that confront you. Instead of Questions for Reflection to end this chapter, please use the reproducible "Building Your Practice of Authentic Reflection" (page 161).

Finally, to continue your journey with the concepts you have learned in book, the reproducible "A Comprehensive Planning Document for Maintaining Your Leadership Capacity" (page 162) will help you develop a yearlong plan for maintaining that capacity.

Building Motivational Clarity Into Your Existing Evaluation Process

Given the importance of maintaining awareness of your authentic sources of volition and motivation, establishing a forum and process for intentional reflection within your existing work environment becomes critical. Use the following to guide you in establishing intentional reflection.

1. Is there a provision for formal reflection included in your current model of professional development or evaluation? If so, will it allow you the time and opportunity to engage in deeper reflection regarding the status of your motivation? If not, how might you construct this opportunity for yourself either within that model or in addition to it?

2. Identify and develop a formal, guided process for reflection that is most meaningful to you. Maintain awareness of your source of volition and motivation in a way that is authentic for you.

3. Does your school or district offer a clear articulation of their expected priorities and values? Do you share these values? These can serve to help you maintain a clear focus of group or team motivation, establishing communication and clarity.

4. Establish and maintain strategies for motivational cueing—authentic representations of your why that you make a part of your physical environment each day. This can include office decor, symbols that are significant to you, or even what you wear.

5. What areas of potential benefit would you like to know more about regarding your efforts to remain connected to your source of motivation? What organizations or activities might support you in remaining connected to your sources of volition? Identify potential areas for extended study or involvement that connect you to these areas.

Building Your Practice of Authentic Reflection

This book has advocated for structured opportunities for authentic reflection in all forms. Authenticity of reflection is an element that runs across all the different elements of developing leadership capacity. Every leader needs the time and space to reflect in a manner that works for them personally. Not everyone is able to access formal meditation or traditional journaling. What is required to be able to reflect in an authentic manner is space, context, and time.

Leaders can do the following.

- Identify the most authentic and productive environment to facilitate their reflection.
- Research and structure the opportunities to engage in that environment on a regular basis.
- Schedule those activities during the most appropriate times of the year, given the demands and opportunities available to them.
- Maintain accountability both for that practice and for the outcomes of that reflection.

Activity	Environment	Opportunity	Times of Year	Outcomes
Structured meditation	Formalized meditation setting	Engage with established protocol or process	Ongoing, periodic	Learn a new approach or connect with an existing one
Outdoor activities	Nature, as is available in your setting	Place yourself in an environment more conducive to reflection	Situational, dependent on climate and surroundings	De-escalation and deeper reflection
Isolated work environment	Removed from regular school setting to engage in a specific task	Greater focus and attention, fewer distractions	Specific projects such as budgeting or planning	A more thoughtful approach to a regular task
Physical exercise	Oriented to type of exercise	Practice physical wellness while freeing head space for deeper thinking	Ongoing, periodic	Direct connection to physical fitness and reflection

Each of these suggestions offers an alternative environment that builds on the idea of authentic reflection and a connection to your ability to engage in your leadership development. The one that works best for you is the one that works best for you. Ultimately, the best choice for you is yours alone.

A Comprehensive Planning Document for Maintaining Your Leadership Capacity

The following template is intended to provide you with an overview of those variables affecting your leadership capacity, resulting in a yearlong plan that can also be used as an addendum to your professional development documents. Set in a competency-based format, it will assist you in developing areas of greatest impact to your own professional development.

Name: _____

Assignment: _____ School Year: _____

Current Areas of Focus: _____

Current Status of Competency by Area: _____

Concentration	Degree of Demonstration				
Physical Well-Being					
Cardiovascular Fitness	0	1	2	3	4
Fitness Activities Scheduled	0	1	2	3	4
Dietary Awareness and Practice	0	1	2	3	4
Management of Physical Symptoms	0	1	2	3	4
Planned Time for Activity	0	1	2	3	4
Fitness Measurement Priorities in Place	0	1	2	3	4
Daily Activity Measurement	0	1	2	3	4
Cognitive and Mental Well-Being					
Sleep Quality and Duration	0	1	2	3	4
De-escalation and Recovery	0	1	2	3	4
Adaptation Strategies in Place	0	1	2	3	4
Emotional Sources of Support					
Awareness of Resources	0	1	2	3	4
Opportunities to Meet Social Needs	0	1	2	3	4
Plan for Support in a Variety of Contexts	0	1	2	3	4
Formal Therapeutic Support in Place	0	1	2	3	4

Motivational Clarity					
Regular Opportunities for Authentic Reflection	0	1	2	3	4
Active Awareness of Volition	0	1	2	3	4
Connections to External Support	0	1	2	3	4

Scale:

0 = Not demonstrated

1 = Started, not yet competent

2 = In progress

3 = Competency demonstrated, ongoing practices

4 = Area of distinction

Artifacts of professional learning: The following activities or outcomes represent your ongoing efforts to maintain your professional capacity. Please feel free to attach additional sheets or artifacts to demonstrate this learning.

1.

2.

3.

Current year goals and areas of focus: In the following figure, please list three areas of focus for the coming school year relative to your efforts to maintain leadership capacity.

Area	Concentration	Goal	Outcome

Areas for continued focus: What areas of well-being and capacity maintenance do you intend to continue prioritizing and practicing?

Physical Well-Being:

Cognitive and Mental Well-Being:

Emotional Sources of Support:

Motivational Clarity:

EPILOGUE

There are many connections between the challenges of maintaining your capacity to lead and those faced by competitive athletes reaching for the upper levels of their sport. Hopefully, you have been able to see and learn from a few of those connections. This book has not examined them all, but those it has can serve as a foundation for a more comprehensive approach to leadership development for your journey going forward.

As is the case with each leader, the path followed by each athlete is theirs alone. They begin with a clear image of their current skill level and build a path upward. Despite the many different programs, resources, and theories, each competitor will have to build their own customized training path to find the outer limits of their abilities. Their path will be ongoing and will adapt over time. It will encompass a range of variables that are defined by what can impact their performance within their sport. They will not stop this pursuit until their volition is either satisfied or extinguished. It is the same with those who lead schools and districts. Every word.

As you prepare to close the back cover of this book and call it read, I want to revisit the parallels between your work and those elements of training from the world of competitive athletes, as outlined in detail in chapter 2 (page 29) that formed the backbone of subsequent chapters. There is much you can learn here.

The following are traits of athletic training programs that can be applied to leadership development.

1. Managing physiological stress reactions
2. Addressing physical, mental, emotional, and motivational variables that impact performance levels
3. Exploring training that is specialized to sport and personalized to athlete
4. Managing physical, cognitive, and emotional energy
5. Using simulation and mental rehearsal
6. Maintaining motivational clarity, which is a clear connection between what you are doing and why you are doing it
7. Using dynamic game planning by planning, planning to adapt, and adapting

School leadership is challenging and unlikely to become easier in the foreseeable future. Therefore, leaders must do more to prepare and sustain themselves under these conditions. It is not a luxury to commit to understanding your own needs for personal well-being. These are foundational elements of optimal performance. They are a part of your responsibility to remain ready to work at your best level as a leader.

As stated throughout this book, the ultimate outcome of this process is for each individual leader to reflect deeply on the elements of their capacity and to structure their own personal approach to maintaining it at optimal levels. Like elite athletes, you must examine the elements of your conditioning that have the greatest potential impact on your performance of day-to-day responsibilities, and structure your approach to training and development to maximize your potential. The good news is that this broader definition will provide significant support to your efforts to remain healthy and effective in this most challenging of leadership environments. The bad news is that, as with elite athletes in competition, you will never arrive at your full potential. Training and development are a journey, not a destination. Even the most seasoned and skilled leaders will always have an element of their capacity that requires work. By acknowledging that and by continuously focusing on your development, you can sustain the energy and effort needed to maintain your level of capacity and lead at the outer limits of your ability.

May you find the energy and support you need to lead on in the best interest of your students.

REFERENCES AND RESOURCES

Albuquerque, T. G., Bragotto, A. P. A., & Costa, H. S. (2022). Processed food: Nutrition, safety, and public health. *International Journal of Environmental Research and Public Health, 19*(24), Article 16410. https://doi.org/10.3390/ijerph192416410

Allostasis. (n.d.). In *Merriam-Webster's online dictionary*. Accessed at www.merriam-webster.com/dictionary/allostasis on August 27, 2024.

AMC Staff. (n.d.). *How being outdoors can relieve stress and anxiety*. Accessed at www.outdoors.org/resources/amc-outdoors/outdoor-resources/how-being-outdoors-can-relieve-stress-and-anxiety on July 2, 2024.

American Psychological Association. (2013, January 1). *How stress affects your health*. Accessed at www.apa.org/topics/stress/health on July 2, 2024.

American Psychological Association. (2018, November 1). *Stress effects on the body*. Accessed at www.apa.org/topics/stress/body on July 2, 2024.

American Psychological Association. (n.d.). *Mindfulness*. Accessed at www.apa.org/topics/mindfulness on March 25, 2024.

Arousal. (2018). In *APA dictionary of psychology*. Accessed at https://dictionary.apa.org/arousal on August 27, 2024.

Attia, P. (Host). (2022, March 28). #201—Deep dive back into zone 2 | Iñigo San-Millán, Ph.D. (Pt. 2) [Audio podcast episode]. In *The Peter Attia drive*. Accessed at https://peterattiamd.com/inigosanmillan2 on July 2, 2024.

Barrett, L. F. (2017a). *How emotions are made: The secret life of the brain*. Boston: Houghton Mifflin Harcourt.

Barrett, L. F. (2017b, December). *You aren't at the mercy of your emotions—your brain creates them*. Accessed at www.ted.com/talks/lisa_feldman_barrett_you_aren_t_at_the_mercy_of_your_emotions_your_brain_creates_them on July 2, 2024.

Barrett, L. F. (2020). *Seven and a half lessons about the brain*. Boston: Houghton Mifflin Harcourt.

Berto, R. (2014). The role of nature in coping with psycho-physiological stress: A literature review on restorativeness. *Behavioral Sciences, 4*(4), 394–409. https://doi.org/10.3390/bs4040394

Boals, A., & Banks, J. B. (2020). Stress and cognitive functioning during a pandemic: Thoughts from stress researchers. *Psychological Trauma: Theory, Research, Practice, and Policy, 12*(S1), S255–S257. https://doi.org/10.1037/tra0000716

Breit, S., Kupferberg, A., Rogler, G., & Hasler, G. (2018). Vagus nerve as modulator of the brain–gut axis in psychiatric and inflammatory disorders. *Frontiers in Psychiatry, 9*. https://doi.org/10.3389/fpsyt.2018.00044

Brower, T. (2022, January 12). *Empathy is the most important leadership skill according to research*. Accessed at www.forbes.com/sites/tracybrower/2021/09/19/empathy-is-the-most-important-leadership-skill-according-to-research on October 8, 2024.

Bryan, L. & Adavadkar, P. (2023, December 14). *Adenosine and sleep: Understanding your sleep drive*. Accessed at www.sleepfoundation.org/how-sleep-works/adenosine-and-sleep on October 4, 2024.

Bryan, L. & Guo, L. (2024, March 15). *Circadian rhythm: What it is, what shapes it, and why it's fundamental to getting quality sleep*. Accessed at www.sleepfoundation.org/circadian-rhythm on March 25, 2024.

Burn, S. M. (2020, October 26). *What does 'allostatic load' mean for your health?* [Blog post]. Accessed at www.psychologytoday.com/us/blog/presence-mind/202010/what-does-allostatic-load-mean-your-health on July 2, 2024.

Calvert, H. (2024, August 9). *The evolution of the marathon world record*. Accessed at https://stories.strava.com/articles/the-evolution-of-the-marathon-world-record on November 13, 2024.

Cardoza, F. (2021, March 17). *Understanding biblical Christian fellowship*. [Blog post.] Accessed at https://seminary.grace.edu/understanding-biblical-christian-fellowship on November 5, 2024.

Center for Science in the Public Interest. (n.d.). *CSPI's food additive safety ratings*. Accessed at www.cspinet.org/page/chemical-cuisine-ratings on February 15, 2024.

Chu, B., Marwaha, K., Sanvictores, T., Awosika, A. O., & Ayers, D. (2024). *Physiology, stress reaction*. Accessed at www.ncbi.nlm.nih.gov/books/NBK541120 on November 5, 2024.

Cleveland Clinic. (n.d.). *Stress.* Accessed at https://my.clevelandclinic.org/health/diseases/11874-stress on October 4, 2024.

Cordova, M. G. (2020, February 25). *Spending time in nature reduces stress, research finds.* Accessed at https://news.cornell.edu/stories/2020/02/spending-time-nature-reduces-stress-research-finds on July 2, 2024.

Diamond, D. M., Campbell, A. M., Park, C. R., Halonen, J., & Zoladz, P. R. (2007). The temporal dynamics model of emotional memory processing: A synthesis on the neurobiological basis of stress-induced amnesia, flashbulb and traumatic memories, and the Yerkes-Dodson law. *Neural Plasticity*, Article 60803. https://doi.org/10.1155/2007/60803

Dimitratos, S. (2018, March 16). *Inflammation: What is it, and how can my diet and behavior affect it?* Accessed at https://nutrition.org/inflammation-what-is-it-and-how-can-my-diet-and-behavior-affect-it on July 2, 2024.

Editors of Encyclopaedia Britannica. (2024, May 27). *Religion.* Accessed at www.britannica.com/topic/religion on July 2, 2024.

Fabritius, F., & Hagemann, H. W. (2017). *The leading brain: Powerful science-based strategies for achieving peak performance.* New York: TarcherPerigee.

Fletcher, E. (2019). *Stress less, accomplish more: Meditation for extraordinary performance.* New York: Morrow.

Freeman, C. R., Zehra, A., Ramirez, V., Wiers, C. E., Volkow, N. D., & Wang, G.-J. (2018). Impact of sugar on the body, brain, and behavior. *Frontiers in Bioscience-Landmark*, *23*(12), 2255–2266. https://doi.org/10.2741/4704

Fridman, L. (Host). (2020, October 4). Lisa Feldman Barrett: Counterintuitive ideas about how the brain works [Audio podcast episode]. In *Lex Fridman podcast.* Accessed at www.youtube.com/watch?v=NbdRIVCBqNI on July 2, 2024.

Fuhrman, J. (2018). The hidden dangers of fast and processed food. *American Journal of Lifestyle Medicine*, *12*(5), 375–381. https://doi.org/10.1177/1559827618766483

Gerritsen, R. J. S., & Band, G. P. H. (2018). Breath of life: The respiratory vagal stimulation model of contemplative activity. *Frontiers in Human Neuroscience*, *12*. https://doi.org/10.3389/fnhum.2018.00397

Goleman, D. (1995). *Emotional intelligence: Why it can matter more than IQ.* New York: Bantam Books.

Guidi, J., Lucente, M., Sonino, N., & Fava, G. A. (2020). Allostatic load and its impact on health: A systematic review. *Psychotherapy and Psychosomatics*, *90*(1), 11–27. https://doi.org/10.1159/000510696

Harvard Health Publishing. (2024, April 3). *Understanding the stress response: Chronic activation of this survival mechanism impairs health.* Accessed at www.health.harvard.edu/staying-healthy/understanding-the-stress-response on July 2, 2024.

Haskell, W. L., Lee, I. M., Pate, R. R., Powell, K. E., Blair, S. N., Franklin, B. A., et al. (2007). Physical activity and public health: Updated recommendation for adults from the American College of Sports Medicine and the American Heart Association. *Medicine and Science in Sports and Exercise, 39*(8), 1423–1434. https://doi.org/10.1249/mss.0b013e3180616b27

Hoffman-Goetz, L., & Pedersen, B. K. (1994). Exercise and the immune system: A model of the stress response? *Immunology Today, 15*(8), 382–387. https://doi.org/10.1016/0167-5699(94)90177-5

Holmes, B. (2022, February 9). *How exercise boosts the brain and improves mental health.* Accessed at www.smithsonianmag.com/science-nature/how-exercise-boosts-the-brain-and-improves-mental-health-180979511 on July 2, 2024.

Huberman, A. (Host). (2021, March 7). Tools for managing stress & anxiety [Audio podcast episode]. In *Huberman lab.* Accessed at www.hubermanlab.com/episode/tools-for-managing-stress-and-anxiety on July 2, 2024.

Huberman, A. (Host). (2022, August 7). Sleep toolkit: Tools for optimizing sleep & sleep-wake timing [Audio podcast episode]. In *Huberman lab.* Accessed at www.hubermanlab.com/episode/sleep-toolkit-tools-for-optimizing-sleep-and-sleep-wake-timing on July 2, 2024.

Intermountain Health. (2020, April 17). *When you're stressed, go outside* [Blog post]. Accessed at https://intermountainhealthcare.org/blogs/when-youre-stressed-go-outside on July 2, 2024.

Jewish Virtual Library. (n.d.). *Jewish dietary laws (Kashrut): Overview of laws and regulations.* Accessed at www.jewishvirtuallibrary.org/overview-of-jewish-dietary-laws-and-regulations on October 15, 2024.

Johnston, W. R., Kaufman, J. H., & Thompson, L. E. (2016, October 31). *Support for instructional leadership: Supervision, mentoring, and professional development for U.S. school leaders—Findings from the American School Leader Panel.* Accessed at www.rand.org/pubs/research_reports/RR1580-1.html on July 2, 2024.

Kabrick, S. (2024, October 4). *11 tips for coping with an anxiety disorder.* Accessed at www.mayoclinichealthsystem.org/hometown-health/speaking-of-health/11-tips-for-coping-with-an-anxiety-disorder on November 11, 2024.

Kanold, T. D. (2017). *HEART! Fully forming your professional life as a teacher and leader.* Bloomington, IN: Solution Tree Press.

Kanold, T. D., & Boogren, T. H. (2022). *Educator wellness: A guide for sustaining physical, mental, emotional, and social well-being.* Bloomington, IN: Solution Tree Press.

King, L. M. (2024, February 12). *What is heart rate variability?* Accessed at www.webmd.com/heart/what-is-heart-rate-variability on November 5, 2024.

Koenig, H. G. (2012). Religion, spirituality, and health: The research and clinical implications. *ISRN Psychiatry*, Article 278730.

Kramer, A. C., Neubauer, A. B., Scott, S. B., Schmiedek, F., Sliwinski, M. J., & Smyth, J. M. (2022). Stressor anticipation and subsequent affective well-being: A link potentially explained by perseverative cognitions. *Emotion*, *22*(8), 1787–1800. https://doi.org/10.1037/emo0000954

Lagos, L. (2020). *Heart breath mind: Train your heart to conquer stress and achieve success.* Boston: Houghton Mifflin Harcourt.

Landry, L. (2019, April 3). *Why emotional intelligence is important in leadership* [Blog post]. Accessed at https://online.hbs.edu/blog/post/emotional-intelligence-in-leadership on December 27, 2023.

Levine, E., & Patrick, S. (2019). *What is competency-based education? An updated definition.* Vienna, VA: Aurora Institute. Accessed at https://aurora-institute.org/wp-content/uploads/what-is-competency-based-education-an-updated-definition-web.pdf on August 27, 2024.

Locus of control. (2013, October 25). In *The Glossary of Education Reform*. Accessed at www.edglossary.org/locus-of-control on July 2, 2024.

Loehr, J., & Groppel, J. (2008). *The corporate athlete advantage: The science of deepening engagement.* Orlando, FL: Human Performance Institute.

Madison, A. A. (2021). Boosting stress resilience using flexibility as a framework to reduce depression risk. *Brain, Behavior, and Immunity—Health*, *18*, Article 100357. https://doi.org/10.1016/j.bbih.2021.100357

Mai, B. H., & Yan, L. J. (2019). The negative and detrimental effects of high fructose on the liver, with special reference to metabolic disorders. *Diabetes, Metabolic Syndrome and Obesity*, *12*, 821–826. https://doi.org/10.2147/DMSO.S198968

Marin, M.-F., Lord, C., Andrews, J., Juster, R.-P., Sindi, S., Arsenault-Lapierre, G., et al. (2011). Chronic stress, cognitive functioning and mental health. *Neurobiology of Learning and Memory*, *96*(4), 583–595. https://doi.org/10.1016/j.nlm.2011.02.016

Martin, M. (2023, December 15). *How to build a sports performance fitness training program.* Accessed at www.acefitness.org/resources/pros/expert-articles/7304/how-to-build-a-sports-performance-fitness-training-program on October 30, 2024.

Maslow, A. H. (1943). A theory of human motivation. *Psychological Review*, *50*(4), 370–396. https://doi.org/10.1037/h0054346

Mayo Clinic Staff. (2022, August 3). *Exercise and stress: Get moving to manage stress.* Accessed at www.mayoclinic.org/healthy-lifestyle/stress-management/in-depth/exercise-and-stress/art-20044469 on July 3, 2024.

Mayo Clinic Staff. (2023a, August 10). *Stress symptoms: Effects on your body and behavior.* Accessed at www.mayoclinic.org/healthy-lifestyle/stress-management/in-depth/stress-symptoms/art-20050987 on October 4, 2024.

Mayo Clinic Staff. (2023b, December 23). *Depression and anxiety: Exercise eases symptoms.* Accessed at www.mayoclinic.org/diseases-conditions/depression/in-depth/depression-and-exercise/art-20046495 on July 3, 2024.

McDonald, E. (2020, September 4). *What foods cause or reduce inflammation?* Accessed at www.uchicagomedicine.org/forefront/gastrointestinal-articles/what-foods-cause-or-reduce-inflammation on December 21, 2023.

McDonogh, D. (n.d.). *How to increase running speed: 8 expert tips.* Accessed at https://vertimax.com/blog/how-to-increase-running-speed on October 2, 2024.

McEwen, B. S. (2000). Allostasis and allostatic load: Implications for neuropsychopharmacology. *Neuropsychopharmacology, 22,* 108–124. https://doi.org/10.1016/S0893-133X(99)00129-3

McLeod, S. (2024, January 24). *Maslow's hierarchy of needs.* Accessed at www.simplypsychology.org/maslow.html on July 3, 2024.

Memorial Sloan Kettering Cancer Center. (2011, July 6). *How fatigue, depression, and other factors affect cognitive function* [Video file]. Accessed at www.youtube.com/watch?v=I3omHkdfzlk on July 3, 2024.

Mendel, B. (n.d.). *Buddhist meditation techniques and practices* [Blog post]. Accessed at https://mindworks.org/blog/buddhist-meditation-techniques-practices on October 15, 2024.

Moriarty, O., McGuire, B. E., & Finn, D. P. (2011). The effect of pain on cognitive function: A review of clinical and preclinical research. *Progress in Neurobiology, 93*(3), 385–404. https://doi.org/10.1016/j.pneurobio.2011.01.002

Moulton, N. H., Fuzi, S. F. S. M., Yussoff, N. E., Shazali, N. M., Mahmud, M. B., & Rahmat, N. H. (2022). Exploring work motivation and work burnout. *International Journal of Academic Research in Business and Social Sciences, 12*(9), 488–507. http://dx.doi.org/10.6007/IJARBSS/v12-i9/11541

National Health Service. (2022, December 16). *5 steps to mental wellbeing.* Accessed at www.nhs.uk/mental-health/self-help/guides-tools-and-activities/five-steps-to-mental-wellbeing on July 3, 2024.

National Institutes of Health. (2019, May 16). *NIH study finds heavily processed foods cause overeating and weight gain.* Accessed at www.nih.gov/news-events/news-releases/nih-study-finds-heavily-processed-foods-cause-overeating-weight-gain on July 3, 2024.

National Policy Board for Educational Administration. (2015). *Professional standards for educational leaders.* Reston, VA: Author. Accessed at www.npbea.org/wp-content/uploads/2017/06/Professional-Standards-for-Educational-Leaders_2015.pdf on July 3, 2024.

National Research Council Committee on Diet, Nutrition, and Cancer. (1983). *Food additives, contaminants, carcinogens, and mutagens.* Washington, DC: National Academies Press. Accessed at www.ncbi.nlm.nih.gov/books/NBK216714 on July 3, 2024.

Nickerson, C. (2023, November 9). *The Yerkes-Dodson law of arousal and performance.* Accessed at www.simplypsychology.org/what-is-the-yerkes-dodson-law.html on July 3, 2024.

Palagi, F. (2024, May 8). *Unveiling the therapy experience: A guide for executives.* Accessed at www.linkedin.com/pulse/unveiling-therapy-experience-guide-executives-felisa-palagi-wbsce on November 5, 2024.

Pate, R. R., Pratt, M., Blair, S. N., Haskell, W. L., Macera, C. A., Bouchard, C., et al. (1995). Physical activity and public health: A recommendation from the Centers for Disease Control and Prevention and the American College of Sports Medicine. *JAMA, 273*(5), 402–407. https://doi.org/10.1001/jama.273.5.402

Patel, J., & Patel, P. (2019). Consequences of repression of emotion: Physical health, mental health and general well being. *International Journal of Psychotherapy Practice and Research, 1*(3), 16–21.

Perna, M. C. (2023, August 2). *Why almost half of school leaders are preparing to call it quits.* Accessed at www.forbes.com/sites/markcperna/2023/08/02/why-almost-half-of-school-leaders-are-preparing-to-call-it-quits on July 3, 2024.

Pietrangelo, A. (2023, March 21). *The effects of stress on your body.* Accessed at www.healthline.com/health/stress/effects-on-body on October 2, 2024.

Roberts, N. F. (2019, March 29). *Science says: Religion is good for your health.* Accessed at www.forbes.com/sites/nicolefisher/2019/03/29/science-says-religion-is-good-for-your-health on July 2, 2024.

Rohleder, N. (2019). Stress and inflammation—The need to address the gap in the transition between acute and chronic stress effects. *Psychoneuroendocrinology, 105*, 164–171. https://doi.org/10.1016/j.psyneuen.2019.02.021

Salleh, M. R. (2008). Life event, stress and illness. *The Malaysian Journal of Medical Sciences, 15*(4), 9–18.

Sapolsky, R. M. (2004). *Why zebras don't get ulcers* (3rd ed.). New York: Times Books.

Shanahan, C. (2020, September 3). *PUFA-project: Scientific references on seed oil toxicity* [Blog post]. Accessed at https://drcate.com/pufa-project on July 2, 2024.

Shanahan, C., & Shanahan, L. (2017). *Deep nutrition: Why your genes need traditional food.* New York: Flatiron Books.

Sinek, S. (2009). *Start with why: How great leaders inspire everyone to take action.* New York: Portfolio.

Sinek, S., Mead, D., & Docker, P. (2017). *Find your why: A practical guide to discovering purpose for you or your team.* New York: Portfolio.

Stephen, F. A., Ermalyn, L. P., Yasmin, M. B., Louise, L. J. D., & Juvenmile, T. B. (2022). A voyage into the visualization of athletic performances: A review. *American Journal of Multidisciplinary Research and Innovation*, 1(3), 105–109. https://doi.org/10.54536/ajmri.v1i3.479

Suni, E., & Vyas, N. (2023, July 18). *How lack of sleep impacts cognitive performance and focus.* Accessed at www.sleepfoundation.org/sleep-deprivation/lack-of-sleep-and-cognitive-impairment on July 3, 2024.

Twohig-Bennett, C., & Jones, A. (2018). The health benefits of the great outdoors: A systematic review and meta-analysis of greenspace exposure and health outcomes. *Environmental Research*, 166, 628–637. https://doi.org/10.1016/j.envres.2018.06.030

U.S. Centers for Disease Control and Prevention. (n.d.). *Get the facts: Added sugars.* Accessed at www.cdc.gov/nutrition/php/data-research/added-sugars.html on July 2, 2024.

U.S. Department of Health and Human Services. (2018). *Physical activity guidelines for Americans* (2nd ed.). Washington, DC: Author. Accessed at https://odphp.health.gov/sites/default/files/2019-09/Physical_Activity_Guidelines_2nd_edition.pdf on November 12, 2024.

U.S. Food and Drug Administration. (2023, June 6). *Types of food ingredients.* Accessed at www.fda.gov/food/food-additives-and-gras-ingredients-information-consumers/types-food-ingredients on July 3, 2024.

Utecht, J. L. (2023, April 5). *Emotional intelligence and adaptability: The key traits to effective leadership.* Accessed at www.linkedin.com/pulse/emotional-intelligence-adaptability-key-traits-jenna-l-utecht-mba on July 3, 2024.

van der Kolk, B. A. (2014). *The body keeps the score: Brain, mind, and body in the healing of trauma.* New York: Viking.

Vander Els, J. G., & Stack, B. M. (2022). *Unpacking the competency-based classroom: Equitable, individualized learning in a PLC at Work.* Bloomington, IN: Solution Tree Press.

Vandrapu, H. (2019, August 22). *Physical fitness is vital to leadership* [Blog post]. Accessed at www.linkedin.com/pulse/physical-fitness-vital-leadership-hari-k-vandrapuu on July 2, 2024.

Velocity Sports Performance. (2021, January 5). *Essential guide to sport-specific training*. Accessed at https://velocityspusa.com/the-essential-guide-to-sport-specific-training on October 13, 2024.

Walker, M. (2017). *Why we sleep: Unlocking the power of sleep and dreams*. New York: Scribner.

Winton, S. L., Palmer, S., & Hughes, P. J. (2018). Developing leadership for increasing complexity: A review of online graduate leadership programs. *Journal of Leadership Education, 17*(1), 162–176.

Yale Medicine. (n.d.). *Chronic stress*. Accessed at www.yalemedicine.org/conditions/stress-disorder on July 3, 2024.

Yaribeygi, H., Panahi, Y., Sahraei, H., Johnston, T. P., & Sahebkar, A. (2017). The impact of stress on body function: A review. *EXCLI journal, 16*, 1057–1072. https://doi.org/10.17179/excli2017-480

Yerkes, R. M., & Dodson, J. D. (1908). The relation of strength of stimulus to rapidity of habit-formation. *Journal of Comparative Neurology and Psychology, 18*(5), 459–482. http://dx.doi.org/10.1002/cne.920180503

INDEX

A
academic model, 9
acetylcholine, 92–93
adaptability, 3
    emotional health and, 109, 112–113
adenosine, 95, 96, 97
allostasis, 55
allostatic load, 53, 54–55
    assessing, 150
    sleep deprivation and, 97
American Heart Association, 78–79
American Psychological Association, 51–52, 57, 60
anxiety, 52–53, 58
arousal, 51–52. *See also* stress
aspirational motivation, 130, 131
assessment
    authentic professional, 11
    competency-based approach and, 40, 41
    embedded, 149
    of leader's present condition, 12
    measuring what matters most in, 37–39
    of physical health, 78, 80, 88–89
    professional development and, 147, 159–160
    of strengths and weaknesses, 150–153
    yearly wellness, 156
athletics
    competency-based approach in, 39–44
    emotional regulation in, 103–105
    energy management in, 91–92
    finding inspiration from training in, 29–48
    measuring what matters in, 37–39
    as model for professional development, 2–3, 5, 7–8, 12–15, 165–166
    motivation in, 125–126
    physical preparation in, 73–74
    planning and practice in, 145–146
    public and organizational perceptions and, 44–45
    speed components in, 35–36
    stress response management and, 49–50
    traits of training programs in, 31–37
attention span, 96–97
Attia, P., 79
Aurora Institute, 40
authenticity, 147–148, 156
    professional assessment and, 11
awareness of others, 113–114

B
Barrett, L. F., 106
belonging, need for, 114–115
blood pressure, 55
brain
    constructed emotion and, 106–107
    rationalization and, 137–138
    sleep and, 92–93, 94–99

breathing, intentional, 99
Brower, T., 113–114
Buddhism, 136
"Building Motivational Clarity Into Your Existing Evaluation Process," 147, 159–160
"Building Your Practice of Authentic Reflection," 158, 161
burnout, 1–2, 8
    motivation and, 127

C

caffeine, 96
capacity
    assessing your, 150–153
    "Capacity Overview Graphic Organizer," 61, 70–72
    cognitive functioning and, 17
    data sources for tracking, 153–155
    focusing on in professional development, 7–27
    leadership ability *vs.*, 14–16
    public and organizational perceptions of, 44–45
    reflection personalization and, 157–158
    skills and attributes and, 20
    stress responses and, 50
    support opportunities and, 155–157
    variables affecting, 19–22
"Capacity Overview Graphic Organizer," 61, 70–72
carbohydrates, 82
cardiovascular health, 59, 76–77, 78–80, 138–139, 153
    inflammation and, 84
"Carving Out Time for Activity," 75, 88
causes, connecting with, 140
challenges, pushing through, 17
Christianity, 136
chronic health conditions, 85
circadian rhythms, 94, 97, 98, 151
cognitive de-escalation, 93–94, 98–99, 151
cognitive functioning, 4, 5
    assessing, 151
    capacity and, 17
    leadership capacity and, 19
    sleep and, 93–94
    stress and, 51, 55
communication, 95, 100
    competency in, 120
    of emotions, 111
    of learning resources, 157
    public and organizational perceptions of, 44–45
    skills for, 36–37
    time management and, 26
competencies
    design principles and, 39–43
    exercise and, 77
    external, 20–21
    internal, 20–21
    professional development based on, 39–44, 147–150
"A Comprehensive Planning Document for Maintaining Your Leadership Capacity," 158, 162–164
comprehensiveness, 12
constructed emotion, 106–107
content, connecting with, 140
context, 12
    for leadership, 128
    reflection and, 138–139
    stress responses and, 63–67
coping skills, 109
Cornell University, 86
cortisol, 53–54, 57, 75–76
COVID-19 pandemic, 1
creativity, 138–139
cross-training, 13–14

D

data sources, 153–155
decision making, 96–97
    motivation and, 137–138
    volition and, 128–130, 142–143
de-escalation, 93–94, 98–99, 120–121, 151
    tracking progress in, 154
design principles, 39–43
diet, 59, 81–84
differentiation, 13, 149
    competency-based approach and, 40, 41, 42
digestive health, 59–60
Dodson, J. D., 52
dopamine, 75–76, 92–93

E

embedded assessment, 149
emotional regulation, 4, 5, 18, 103–123

assessing your capacity in, 151–152
in athletics, 103–105
emotional health and, 109–115
leadership capacity and, 19–20
mental rehearsal, simulations, and, 105, 120–121
reflection on, 118–119
in school, 106–109
stress and, 55
support systems and, 105
tracking progress in, 154–155
empathy, 109–110, 113–114
employee services, 117–118
employee support systems, 117–118
empowerment, 40, 41
Encyclopedia Britannica, 135
endorphins, 86
energy, 3, 32–33
assessing, 150
comparing benefit and expenditure of, 43–44
sleep and, 91–102
engagement, 52–53
equity, 40, 42
exercise, 59, 77–80, 138–139
expectations, 14, 100
competency-based approach and, 40, 43
measuring performance and, 38
motivation and, 131–133
experience, value of, 107
extrinsic motivation, 129, 131

F

Fabritius, F., 92–93
Fadare, S. A., 108
faith, 135–136
family, 140
fatigue, 100–101. *See also* sleep
fight or flight, 53–54, 75–76, 83
fitness trackers, 79–80
Fletcher, E., 158
focus
in athletic training, 13–14
fractured, in leadership development, 11
sleep deprivation and, 95
Forbes, 8
framing, leadership capacity and, 16

friends, 140
fulfillment, 114

G

glucose, 76–77, 81–82
glycation, 82
goals, 38–39, 152
group therapy, 117
gut health, 59–60

H

Hagemann, H. W., 92–93
health, emotional, 109–115
health, physical, 17, 18
annual examinations and, 37
assessing, 150
exercise and, 59, 77–80
leadership capacity and, 19–20
long-term stress and, 54–55
making time for, 75, 90
outdoor time and, 85–86, 140
sickness and, 84–85
sleep and, 91–102
stress and, 57–61
"The Health Benefits of the Great Outdoors" (National Institutes of Health), 86
health insurance, 117–118
heart rate variability (HRV), 78–79
hierarchy of needs, 114–115
historical motivation, 130, 131
How Emotions Are Made: The Secret Life of the Brain (Barrett), 106
Hughes, P. J., 11

I

"Identifying your Essential Competencies," 22, 26–27
immune system, 76, 83, 86
individual therapy, 117
inflammation, 76, 83–84
insulin, 81–82
intentional breathing, 99
interoception, 85, 106, 139–140
intrinsic motivation, 129, 131
"An Inventory of How You Are Feeling," 80, 89–90
"An Inventory of Work Challenges," 18, 24–25

J

Judaism, 136
judgment, 96–97
    motivation and, 133–135
Juvenmile, T. D., 108

L

Lambaco, E., 108
leaders and leadership
    capacity *vs.* ability in, 14–16
    contexts for, 128
    emotion expression by, 110–112
    expanded responsibilities in, 8, 10–11
    focusing on capacity for, 7–27
    personalized plans for, 6
    positional, 128
    preparation for, 5
    public and organizational perceptions of, 44–45
    situational, 128
    state of development for, 9–12
    subskills for, 35–37
    sustaining, 30–31
    varying skills and abilities for, 34–35
The Leading Brain: Powerful Science-Based Strategies for Achieving Peak Performance (Fabritius & Hagemann), 92–93
learning
    cataloging resources for, 157
    competency-based, 39–44
    professional learning days, 149
life situations, motivation and, 133, 134–135
Louise, L. J. D., 108

M

"Maintaining Emotional Supports Graphic Organizer," 114, 122–123
Mangorsi, Y. B., 108
McDonald, E., 83
McEwen, B. S., 55
meditation, 99, 136, 157, 158
memories, motivation and, 131–133
Mendel, B., 136
mental capacity, assessing your, 151
mental conditioning programs, 3–4
mental rehearsal, 3, 33, 103–105, 108, 120–121
    assessing your capacity for, 152
    facilitated, 156
    tracking your progress in, 154
metrics and measurement, 37–39, 153–155
    for physical health, 78–79
mindfulness, 60–61, 99, 136, 157–158
    spirituality and, 135–136
mindsets, 17
    workaholic, 74
motivation, 3, 4, 5–6, 125–143
    aspirational *vs.* historical, 130, 131
    assessing your capacity for, 152
    in athletics, 125–126
    clarity in, leadership capacity and, 20, 155, 156–157
    exercise and, 79
    intrinsic *vs.* extrinsic, 129, 131
    locating your, 131–135
    maintaining clarity in, 33–34
    positive *vs.* negative, 130, 131
    purpose and, 127–130, 139–141
    reflection and, 137–139, 141
    source chart, 131
    spirituality and, 135–136
    volition and, 128, 133–134

N

National Institutes of Health, 86
needs, social, 114–115
negative motivation, 130, 131
norepinephrine, 75–76, 92–93

O

oils, healthy, 82–83
O'Masta, L., 8
ongoing development, 12
orientation, 9
outdoors, spending time in, 85–86, 140

P

Palmer, S., 11
parachute phrases, 100
parasympathetic nervous system, 78–79, 98–99, 151
Patel, J., 111
Patel, P., 111
"A Path to Mindfulness, Authentic Reflection, and Self-Awareness," 60, 68–69
performance, optimal, 2
    athletics as a model for, 7–8, 12–15
    examining variables affecting, 14–18

measuring what matters and, 37–39
putting it into practice, 145–164
sleep and, 91–102
stress and, 52–53
variables affecting, 2, 32
Perna, M. C., 8
personalization, 6, 9, 13, 32, We 165
in athletic training, 12
competency-based approach and, 39–44
lack of in traditional development, 10
planning and implementing, 147–150
of reflection, 157–158
physical preparation, 73–90. *See also* health, physical
assessing, 150
in athletics, 73–74
diet and, 81–84
exercise and, 59, 77–80
outdoor time and, 85–86
sickness and, 84–85
sleep and, 91–102
for stress responses, 75–77
Pietrangelo, A., 50
planning, 34, 145–146
emotional regulation and, 107–109
professional development and, 147–150
positional leadership, 128
positive motivation, 130, 131
practice, 145–164
procedures, for professional development, 148–149
processed food, 81
professional associations, 117
professional development, 2
athletic training and, 2–3, 5, 7–8, 12–15, 29–48, 165–166
competency-based, 20–22
competency-based approach to, 147–150
current state of, 9–12
data for tracking, 153–155
focusing on capacity in, 7–27
as journey *vs.* destination, 166
motivation and, 141
personalized planning for, 6
putting it into practice, 145–164
strengths/weaknesses assessment and, 150–153
support opportunities and, 155–157
progress. *See also* metrics and measurement
competency-based approach and, 41–42
data sources for tracking, 153–155
"Protocol for Building the Work in the Current System," 47–48
protocols, 100
public perceptions, 118
purpose, motivation and, 127–130, 134–135, 139–141
spirituality and, 135–136

R

RAND Corporation, 9
rationalization, 137
reflection, 6, 152
on athletic training approaches, 46
authentic, 156, 161
on emotional regulation, 118–119
emotional regulation and, 107
environments conducive to, 138–139
on leadership capacity and development, 26–27
mindfulness and, 60, 68–69
motivation and, 137–139, 141
personalizing your approach to, 157–158
on physical preparation, 86–87
on sleep, 101
on stress responses, 61–62
tracking progress in, 154
relaxation techniques, 99
religion, 135–136
reproducibles
"A Comprehensive Planning Document for Maintaining Your Leadership Capacity," 158, 162–164
"A Path to Mindfulness, Authentic Reflection, and Self-Awareness," 60, 68–69
"An Inventory of How You Are Feeling," 80, 89–90
"An Inventory of Work Challenges," 18, 24–25
"Building Motivational Clarity Into Your Existing Evaluation Process," 147, 159–160

"Building Your Practice of Authentic Reflection," 158, 161
"Capacity Overview Graphic Organizer," 61, 70–72
"Carving Out Time for Activity," 75, 88
"Identifying your Essential Competencies," 22, 26–27
"Maintaining Emotional Supports Graphic Organizer," 114, 122–123
"Protocol for Building the Work in the Current System," 47–48
"Sleep Hygiene Checklist," 95, 102
"Uncovering Your Volition," 130, 142–143
"Understanding the Context of Your Stress Reactions," 63–67
"Using Mental Rehearsal and Simulation to Prepare for Escalated Emotional Response," 105, 120–121
resilience, 17–18. *See also* capacity
physical, 79–80
retreats, 149
role models, 17

S

sacrifice, 17–18
San-Millán, I., 79
self-actualization, 109
therapeutic support and, 116
self-awareness, 18
emotional health and, 109
emotional regulation and, 110–112
fatigue and, 100
motivation and, 128–129
sickness and, 85
sleep and, 97–98, 100–101
stress management and, 61
self-care, 2
self-interest, 137–138
selflessness, 141
self-management, 109, 110–112
sensory neurons, 99
simulations, 3, 33, 103–105, 120–121
emotional regulation and, 107–109
Sinek, S., 128–129
situational leadership, 128
skills and abilities, 34–36
sleep
assessing, 151
the brain and, 92–93, 94–98
de-escalation and, 93–94, 98–99
duration *vs.* quality of, 94–95
fatigue and, 100–101
reflections on, 101
tracking progress in, 154
sleep aids, 97
sleep hygiene, 95
"Sleep Hygiene Checklist," 95, 102
social needs, 114–115, 151
social skills, 109–110, 113–114
specialization, 13, 32
spirituality, 135–136
Stack, B. M., 39–40
standards, professional development based on, 9–10, 11
Start With Why: How Great Leaders Inspire Everyone to Take Action (Sinek), 128–129
stress
assessing your reactions to, 152
de-escalation and, 93–94, 98–99, 105, 151
emotional regulation and, 107–108
fight or flight and, 53–54
health, illness, and, 57–61
long-term, 54–55
managing physiological reactions to, 2, 5, 31–32, 49–72
outdoor time and, 86
perceptions of, 55–57
physical preparation for, 75–77
positive aspects of, 51
putting and, 49–50
sleep and, 92–93
understanding reactions to, 51–57
Stress Less, Accomplish More: Meditation for Extraordinary Performance (Fletcher), 158
students, connecting with, 139–140
subskills, 35–37
suffering, 17–18
sugar, 81–82
support systems, 105, 111–112, 114, 122–123, 151, 152
finding opportunities with, 155–157
therapeutic, 116–118
sympathetic nervous system, 53–54, 57, 58, 75–76, 78–79, 151

T

tapping out, 101
therapeutic support, 116–118
time, outdoor, 85–86, 140
time management, 26, 147–150

U

"Uncovering Your Volition," 130, 142–143
"Understanding the Context of Your Stress Reactions," 63–67
University of New Hampshire, 3–4
Unpacking the Competency-Based Classroom: Equitable, Individualized Learning in a PLC at Work (Vander Els & Stack), 39–40
"Using Mental Rehearsal and Simulation to Prepare for Escalated Emotional Response," 105, 120–121

V

vagus nerve, 99
values
    assessments and, 37–38
    motivation and, 134–135
Vander Els, J. G., 39–40
visualization, 3, 33, 108

volition, 5–6, 128. *See also* motivation
    adapting to changes in, 134–135
    recovering from loss of, 133–134
    spirituality and, 135–136
    supporting, 152

W

Walker, M., 94–95, 96–97
weight loss, 84
well-being, 4, 16–17. *See also* emotional regulation
    community and organizational perceptions of efforts around, 45
    leadership capacity and, 19
    physical, 73–87
    tracking progress in, 154
wellness evaluations, 156
Winton, S. L., 11
workaholic mindset, 74
workshops, 149
worry, 58

Y

Yerkes, R. M., 52
Yerkes-Dodson Law, 52–53

Teaching Self-Regulation
Amy S. Gaumer Erickson and Patricia M. Noonan
Self-regulation fuels students to become socially and emotionally engaged, lifelong learners. With this timely resource you'll gain 75 instructional activities to teach self-regulation in any secondary classroom. Ample teacher-tested tools and templates are also included to help you create authentic learning experiences and deliver effective feedback.
BKF988

Motivated to Learn
Staci M. Zolkoski, Calli Lewis Chiu, and Mandy E. Lusk
In *Motivated to Learn*, you will gain evidence-based approaches for engaging students and equipping them to better focus in the classroom. With this book's straightforward strategies, you can learn to motivate all your students to actively participate in learning.
BKG037

The Metacognitive Student
Richard K. Cohen, Deanne Kildare Opatosky, James Savage, Susan Olsen Stevens, and Edward P. Darrah
What if there was one strategy you could use to support students academically, socially, and emotionally? It exists—and it's simple, straightforward, and practical. Dive deep into structured SELf-questioning and learn how to empower students to develop into strong, healthy, and confident thinkers.
BKF954

Brick by Brick
Kjell Fenn
Using research-supported strategies, author Kjell Fenn guides new teachers through four pillars of successful teaching: planning, structure, engagement, and confidence. Learn how to design assessments, craft lesson plans, and find the structure for students and teachers to experience joy in the classroom.
BKG214

Visit SolutionTree.com or call 800.733.6786 to order.

Wait! Your professional development journey doesn't have to end with the last pages of this book.

We realize improving student learning doesn't happen overnight. And your school or district shouldn't be left to puzzle out all the details of this process alone.

No matter where you are on the journey, we're committed to helping you get to the next stage.

Take advantage of everything from **custom workshops** to **keynote presentations** and **interactive web and video conferencing**. We can even help you develop an action plan tailored to fit your specific needs.

Let's get the conversation started.

Call 888.763.9045 today.

SolutionTree.com